A Postcard from the Fifties

Best Wishes

Gillian Jackson

Gillian Jackson

A portrait of a momentous decade through the medium of picture postcards. Over 270 cards show the fashions, events, transport and humour of the 1950s

ISBN I 900138 29 8
Designed and published by Reflections of a Bygone Age, Keyworth, Nottingham 2002

Printed by Adlard Print and Reprographics Ltd, Ruddington, Notts

For a full list of books from Reflections of a Bygone Age, please write to 15 Debdale Lane, Keyworth, Nottingham NG12 5HT, or ring 0115 937 4079. We also publish a monthly magazine for postcard collectors.

£7.95

Gillian Jackson was born in Lichfield, Staffordshire, and moved to North Wales as a child. Married to Trevor, she has two sons, Richard and Michael. Her interest in picture postcards started with a shoebox full that were given to her when she was a youngster - part of her grandmother's collection. Once she discovered postcard fairs, Gillian's collection grew, and she developed a particular enthusiasm for cards of the 1950s and 1960s. She has written many articles for *Picture Postcard Monthly*, and co-authored two books on Chester. She is a founder-member of both Chester and Wirral Postcard Clubs.

Postcard collecting has become one of Britain's favourite collecting hobbies. All the rage in Edwardian Britain, it was reborn in the 1960s when original albums began to come onto the market, and collectors rediscovered the unique appeal and charm of picture postcards. Much of this appeal is based on nostalgia, though picture postcards are multi-faceted. They offer a range of subjects and places which have the potential to interest virtually anyone. They are important for historians of all kinds - military, social and family - and to industrial archaeologists. Postcards often feature photographs which cannot be sourced elsewhere.

Top publishers: The postcards in this book are the work of a large number of different publishers. Pre-eminent in the fifties were Raphael Tuck of London, Bamforth of Holmfirth, Valentine of Dundee and Francis Frith of Reigate, all of whom had picture postcard credentials stretching back to the end of the 19th century. Tuck were top publishers in the Golden Age (1900-14), when they produced cards of high quality and promoted prize competitions to an eager public hooked on the bug of collecting picture postcards. National publishers in the fifties concentrated on scenes and events that would be popular with tourists, though many postcards were issued by businesses as promotional items. In this decade there were fewer small local publishers, which half a century earlier had focused on more parochial events. Where known, card publishers are noted within the captions.

THE WHITE ROSE.

The Class A3 locomotive, No.60046, *Diamond Jubilee*, is seen leaving Leeds for London, King's Cross, in the mid-fifties. The engine is producing so much smoke that it almost obliterates the signals on the gantry as it passes beneath. The driver is leaning out of his cab, watching the photographer. *(Published by Valentine & Sons Ltd., real photograph no. RP63).*

THE EVERLY BROTHERS

With their unique harmonies and clean-cut looks, the Everly Brothers were the subject of much teenage adulation. They had changed their country and western style of singing for tuneful versions of rock 'n' roll songs, and were soon in great demand. Their first big hit was *Bye Bye Love* in 1957, followed by *Wake Up Little Susie*. They topped the British charts twice in 1958 with *All I have to do is Dream* and *Bird Dog,* and finished the decade with *'Til I Kissed You*, which reached no. 2. The Everlys went on to even greater success in the 1950s. *(Real photograph no. 761 by anonymous publisher).*

BIRMINGHAM NEW STREET

A Postcard from the Fifties

CONTENTS

Acknowledgments:
This book would not have been possible without the support of my family and the publishers. I am especially grateful to my son Michael, who spent many hours deciphering my handwriting and typing out the first draft.

Birmingham's New Street has now been largely pedestrianised, but in the late fifties walkers ruled the area anyway. The writer of the postcard, sent to Cardiff, explains: *"went for a run to Coventry last evening to see Cathedral, only 35 minutes by car. We are going to Stratford-on-Avon this afternoon, which is only half an hour's run."* (no. 12 in a series by unidentified publisher).

INTRODUCTION

The 1950s was an exciting decade for many people. I remember the thrill of seeing my first television programme on a neighbour's set, travelling in our own car, listening to the new "pop" stars - and starting my postcard collection! In 1951, at the age of six, I was given a shoebox full of old postcards that had belonged to my grandmother - little did they know what they were starting! I was fascinated by these pictures and was soon adding to the box as family and friends kept me supplied. Since then, the collection has grown to fill several boxes and albums.

Picture postcards first appeared in Britain in 1894, when a small picture shared the front with any correspondence and the back was reserved for the address. From 1902, the back was divided for both address and correspondence so that the picture could take up the whole of the front. From this date until 1918, the output of cards was prolific, and collecting became a national craze. Today's collectors refer to this period as the Golden Age of Postcards. After 1918, a rise in postage rates and greater use of the telephone led to a decline in the hobby. Collecting postcards became popular again in the 1970s and is now second only to stamps.

Although postcards were not issued in such great numbers between 1918-1970, there is still a wide variety of subjects to collect as well as the usual scenic types. In the 1950s, I received many cards designed especially for children as well as comic ones, views of the latest ships, trains and planes, personalities, royalty and events. I am still adding to the collection by searching at postcard and antique fairs and collectors' shops.

This book is an attempt to look at life in the 1950s through the medium of postcards in my collection. I have, therefore, only been able to illustrate subjects that the postcard publishers thought suitable for publication. The happier events such as the Coronation and Festival of Britain received wide coverage, with hundreds of different designs, but the wars and disasters of the 1950s rarely appeared on postcards, and nor did politicians! Specialist publishers also issued many cards showing clean-cut images of film and "pop" stars but cards of "teddy boys" and coffee bars are rare.

The cards are arranged thematically and a closer inspection of many of the views will reveal a wealth of detail that there is no room to mention in the text. Where appropriate, details of messages and postal usage are given. Cards posted in the 1960s are examples of fifties' views that were still being sold in later years. For fellow collectors, details of the publishers - if known - are given in brackets at the end of each entry.

I hope the selection will evoke happy memories for many readers and, for those who are too young to remember, I hope it will give an interesting glimpse of that period of your parents' or grandparents' lives.

Gillian Jackson
April 2002

One of my first cards, a Mabel Lucie Attwell design that was sent to me because I enjoyed her books. *(Posted in Mold, December, 1951; published by Valentine & Sons Ltd., no. 1662).*

Main Street, Ravenglass, with a garage and petrol station on the left. *(Published by Sankeys Ltd., real photograph no. H709/R).*

The Fifties – a decade of change

This was a period of great change in the British way of life. On New Year's Day, 1950, Britons were struggling to cope with post-war austerity and rationing – with shortages more acute than during the actual war years. Gradually, such hardship became just a memory. As rationing was phased out and factory production increased, the shops were able to stock their shelves once more and there was a boom in sales of everything from food to cars. For housewives, shopping for food was continually changing. Supermarkets and self-service shops employed fewer staff, so most items had to be pre-packaged. There was a wider choice – especially of convenience foods – as customers were keen to try more foreign recipes and foodstuffs advertised on the new commercial TV channel. Refrigerators enabled people to store food for longer and so shop less often – and the small ice-box compartment could take a couple of the latest "TV dinners". Also on the domestic front, electrical appliances were cheaper and better-designed, so that many families eagerly purchased their first vacuum cleaner, washing machine, spin dryer and the smaller labour-saving items such as irons, kettles, food mixers and saucepans protected with the innovative non-stick coating. In many living rooms, the chairs were no longer arranged around the hearth but were placed to face a television set.

At work, automation and modern machinery led to greater efficiency and a cleaner working environment. There was a growth in most manufacturing and service industries, but particularly in cars, food and drug manufacture and in banking, insurance and building societies. With business booming, there was no shortage of jobs, both full and part time, and wives were tempted to go out to work as well. A wife's wages were often saved to pay for the luxuries that soon became the norm – new houses, central heating, cars and holidays. The end of petrol rationing heralded a boom in private motoring and the Highway Code was frequently amended as new rules were required to keep all these new motorists in order!

People also travelled further afield as package holidays and colourful brochures encouraged them to widen their horizons. The new jet airliners shortened journey times and, by 1959, passengers were choosing to travel by air instead of the more restful sea voyage on a luxurious passenger liner. To take a car to the continent, there were air ferries and roll-on, roll-off ships were introduced. The prototype hovercraft was demonstrated to a fascinated crowd of onlookers in 1959. On the railways, diesel and electric locomotives gradually replaced the steam engines – but steam enthusiasts founded the first of several preservation societies at Talyllyn. In towns with a surviving tramway system, the trams were replaced by trolleybuses and motorbuses so that trams were a rare sight by 1959.

The British landscape was transformed when new building regulations allowed the construction of high-rise buildings for both office and residential use. However, it was decided to preserve the best of the country's landscape and the first National Park – the Peak District – was designated in 1950 and the first Area of Outstanding Natural Beauty – the Gower Peninsula – was designated in 1956. The Festival of Britain, in 1951, was intended to promote Britain, stimulate trade and be a "tonic to the nation". The exhibits displayed the British way of life and achievements in the arts, science and technology. As the decade progressed, there were many more technological developments. Everyone benefitted from the introduction of those miniature marvels, the transistor and microchip. Electricity was generated by nuclear power – with Britain's Calder Hall power station being the first in the world. Satellites were developed for use in meteorology, communication and broadcasting. On a smaller scale there was the introduction of video machines, music synthesisers, float glass and fibre optics. In the world of medicine, there were many life-saving developments with the first heart pacemaker, kidney transplant, radiation treatment and polio vaccine. Space travel, dismissed by many in 1950 as being pure science fiction had become a reality by 1959.

All over the world, human achievements were surpassing all expectations and to chart these events, the first *Guinness Book of Records* was published in 1955. Sportsmen, making full use of better training facilities, constantly set new records. It was a great day for British athletics when Roger Bannister became the first man to run a mile in under four minutes in 1954. Explorers and mountaineers were able to take advantage of lighter equipment and better materials for tents, clothes and boots, which helped them achieve some notable conquests. The first crossing of the Antarctic was completed in 1958, by a party led by Dr. Vivian Fuchs. The world's three highest peaks were all conquered; the highest, Mount Everest, was first when Edmund Hillary and Sherpa Tensing reached the summit in 1953; the next highest K2, was conquered by an Italian party in 1954 and the third highest, Kangchenjunga, was conquered by a British party in 1955.

News of the conquest of Everest reached Britain at the time of the Coronation, when the country was celebrating the beginning of a new Elizabethan Age. The young royal family were greeted enthusiastically wherever they went and the progress of the young prince and princess was watched with interest. For all children, the decade was to be a momentous one. Comprehensive education was phased in by many local authorities and the GCE "O" and "A" level examinations were introduced. However, the greatest change of all was the emergence of the "teenager". The title was not used until the 1950s, when this age group devised their own culture. As there were plenty of jobs for youngsters, they had money to spend on clothes, cigarettes, cinema, dancing and the new 45 rpm records to play on their portable record players. Rock 'n' Roll was their own music and they jived to the latest skiffle groups or listened to records on the juke box, as they sipped frothy coffee in the local coffee bar. The girls wore full skirts over layers of net petticoats and the boys wore suits reminiscent of the Edwardian era, gaining the nickname "teddy boys".

On December 31st 1959, as the chimes of Big Ben signalled the end of the 1950s, it did not seem possible that so much could have taken place in the space of a mere ten years.

High Street, Melksham - when parking was easy! *(Published by Thames Valley Associated Press, series no. 2569).*

To mark the centenary of Big Ben in 1959, this special card was issued giving details of the famous clock and its mechanism. *(Published by Raphael Tuck & Sons Ltd.)*

The Royal Family

As the decade dawned, the British Royal Family was headed by the 54-year old King George VI and his wife, Queen Elizabeth. The King's mother, Queen Mary, was 82 years old but still fairly active. Princess Elizabeth, the heir to the throne, had been married to the Duke of Edinburgh for just over two years and their son, Prince Charles, was a year old. Princess Margaret, aged 19, was a society beauty and a popular guest at both public and private functions.

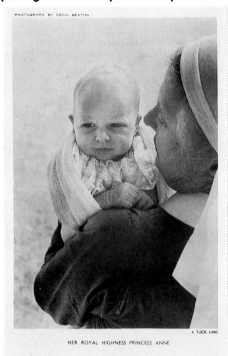

HER ROYAL HIGHNESS PRINCESS ANNE

· In · Memoriam ·

His late Majesty King George VI.

Born December 14th, 1895.
Ascended the Throne December 11th, 1936.
Passed peacefully away February 6th, 1952.

104B

There was a new addition to the Royal Family with the birth of Princess Anne on 15th August 1950, at Clarence House. Here, the royal infant is seen with her nurse. *(Published by Raphael Tuck & Sons Ltd., real photograph no.A4. Photo by Cecil Beaton).*

The nation was shocked and saddened by the untimely death of George VI. He died of cancer at Sandringham on 6th February 1952. On the back of this "In Memoriam" card, there is the phrase *"With gratitude for the Past and a wish for the Future".* (Published by Raphael Tuck & Sons Ltd., real photograph no.104B).

LONDON'S FAREWELL TO KING GEORGE VI.
THE FUNERAL TRAIN ABOUT TO LEAVE PADDINGTON
DRAWN BY THE "WINDSOR CASTLE"

The King's body was taken by train to London. At every rail crossing, crowds waited to pay their last respects as the train passed at a slow 20 m.p.h. The body lay in state in Westminster Hall and over 300,000 people filed past. The funeral took place on 15th February when the coffin was carried on a gun-carriage through the streets of London to Paddington Station. The funeral train took the coffin, together with members of the Royal Family and political leaders, to Windsor, where the King was laid to rest in the vault of St. George's Chapel. The funeral was broadcast by BBC radio. *(Published by Raphael Tuck & Sons Ltd., real photograph no.107A).*

First televised Coronation

It was the first Coronation to be televised and for many people, it was their first experience of television. Those with sets re-arranged furniture to squeeze as many people as possible into their front rooms: children had to sit on the floor. The broadcast began at 10 a.m. and went on until 11.30 p.m. Mealtimes were arranged so as not to clash with the crucial moments, and the voice of Richard Dimbleby added to the ceremony of the occasion. The following day was a holiday and street parties were held throughout the land. It was the first major event to be broadcast internationally.

CHT 5
THE SCENE IN WESTMINSTER ABBEY AT THE CORONATION
OF HER MAJESTY QUEEN ELIZABETH, JUNE 2ND, 1953
A TUCK CARD

The most mystical and sacred part of the Coronation ceremony is the anointing. The Queen, divested of her crimson robe, sits in King Edward's Chair. Just visible above her is the canopy of golden cloth, held by four Knights of the Garter, which is used to screen her from general view. The Archbishop then anoints her with holy oil on her hand, breast and forehead. *(Published by Raphael Tuck & Sons Ltd., no.CHT 5).*

Once back at the Palace, numerous photographs were taken. This one shows the Queen, wearing St. Edward's Crown, with her six maids of honour and the Mistress of the Robes, the Dowager Duchess of Devonshire. The Maids of Honour wore dazzling white dresses with golden sequins, and their duty was to carry the Queen's long train. The postcard is one of a "Coronation Souvenir" series published by Valentines of Dundee. On the reverse of the card, they explain that the prints were flown to their studios in Dundee for processing and the postcards were on sale in London by 11 a.m. on June 3rd. *(Published by Valentine & Sons Ltd., real photograph no.C47).*

Despite the unseasonable weather – it was cold and wet – over 130,000 people camped out along the route of the procession for the whole night before Coronation Day. It was worth the wait as marching bands, servicemen, and coach after coach passed by, at walking pace, on the way to the Abbey. The coaches carried various members of the Royal Family and Prime Ministers of the Commonwealth, before the Queen arrived in the golden State Coach at exactly 11 a.m. after the 35-minute drive. The Coronation service was conducted by the Archbishop of Canterbury. When the newly-crowned Queen emerged from the Abbey, the waiting crowds watched the whole procession retrace its journey to Buckingham palace. Later, there was an RAF flypast, watched by the whole Royal Family from the Palace balcony. The Queen and Duke made several appearances on the balcony that evening, waving to the cheering crowds below. The Mall was floodlit and the Royal couple made their final appearance at midnight.

THE QUEEN WITH HER MAIDS OF HONOUR
C.47.

H 4
THE ROYAL HOMECOMING
BRITANNIA PASSES UNDER TOWER BRIDGE
A TUCK CARD

After the Coronation, the Queen and the Duke of Edinburgh made special visits to Wales, Scotland, and Northern Ireland. In January 1954, they embarked on a long Round the World Tour when they visited most of the Commonwealth countries. Their return on 15th May 1954 was quite an occasion. They arrived in the new *Britannia,* and were accompanied by a waterway procession of smaller boats. Later, the Royal Family waved to the crowds from the balcony of Buckingham Palace. *(Posted in London July 1954; published by Raphael Tuck & Sons Ltd., real photograph no.H4).*

During Coronation Year, collectors of Royalty memorabilia were confronted by a vast range of commemorative items and many new collectors were 'hooked'. Scrapbooks were quickly filled with cuttings from newspapers and magazines. People were particularly interested in the Royal children and, to meet the demand, postcard publishers issued many cards featuring Charles and Anne, showing their progress over the decade.

On the left, the newly-proclaimed Queen poses with her young children. Princess Anne was probably restless as she is holding what looks like a saucer and key ring, to keep her occupied. (Real photograph by Marcus Adams, no.699).

A year later, the children were shown in a series of delightful poses whilst examining the workings of the photographer's watch – seen in Charles' hand here. (Real photograph by Marcus Adams, no.716).

This informal study was taken by photographer Lisa Sheridan who held a royal warrant from the Queen Mother, seen here keeping her young grandchildren amused. (Published by Raphael Tuck & Sons Ltd., real photograph no.129D).

In July 1958, Prince Charles was created the Prince of Wales by the Queen. Here he is seen with his sister, with the Royal train in the background. (Lansdowne Publishing Co. Ltd., real photograph).

Another Lisa Sheridan photo, showing Prince Charles with one of the Queen Mother's corgis. (Raphael Tuck no.129F).

Princess Anne's love of horses started early. Here, she already seems confident and capable of helping the Queen with this pony at Balmoral. (Posted in London, May 1956; published by Valentine & Sons Ltd., real photograph no. 36/5).

Despite the numerous tours, visits and state occasions attended by the Royal family, few postcards show these events but concentrate on formal portraits, and family groups. After the sudden death of her father, the Queen and her husband were thrown into a whirl of Royal assignments, visiting all corners of the Commonwealth. They were also coping with the demands of a changing world and the ever present eye of the T.V. camera. After the international success of the coronation broadcasts, many events were televised and, in 1957, the Queen recorded the first televised Royal Christmas message. The presentations of debutantes was felt to be an archaic practice in the new Elizabethan age and the final 'curtsey to the Queen' was held in March 1958. The decade ended on a high note for the Royal family when it was announced that the Queen was expecting a child early in 1960.

Prince Philip is credited with having suggested many of the changes that updated the image of the Royal family and increased their involvement with charitable organisations and the outside world. It was his idea to encourage the country's youth to make the most of their time and opportunities and so, in February, 1956, he announced details of his Duke of Edinburgh Award Scheme. He was delighted to award the first Gold Medals, in a ceremony at Buckingham Palace, in June 1958. The Scheme has gone from strength to strength since then. *(Real photograph by Baron, no.710).*

H.M. THE QUEEN AND H.R.H. THE DUKE OF EDINBURGH 713

When using the royal car on a visit, the Royal couple would be driven slowly past the cheering crowds so that everyone should be able to see them properly. To give her subjects a better view, the car had wide windows, a glass roof, and a rear screen that could be folded down in fine weather. *(Real photograph no.713 by anonymous publisher).*

H.R.H. THE PRINCESS MARGARET

The radiant beauty of Princess Margaret that so attracted Group Captain Peter Townsend. Romance blossomed between them but, as he had been divorced, he was not considered to be a suitable husband for the Princess. In October, 1955, she took the painful decision not to marry him. *(Published by Raphael Tuck & Sons Ltd., real photograph no.90B).*

This postcard shows the couple in evening dress, but no mention is made of the function they were attending. *(Published by Photographic Greeting Card Co. Ltd., real photograph no.RF58).*

Princess Margaret carried out her share of Royal duties, as here on a visit to Llandaff Cathedral in February 1958. She is accompanied by the Bishop of Llandaff, the Rt. Rev. W.G.H. Simon and other local dignitaries. *(Photo by Western Mail).*

Festival of Britain

In 1947, it was decided to mark the centenary of the Great Exhibition of 1851 with a festival of national displays of the Arts, Architecture, Sciences, Technology and Industrial Design. It was also intended to be a 'tonic to the nation', which was still suffering from the after-effects of World War 2, and hopefully, would encourage creativity and stimulate trade. A derelict, bomb-damaged area on the South Bank was chosen for the main site and despite problems with supplies, trade unions and the weather, the Festival was completed within its budget (of £8 million) and opened on time. The Opening Ceremony took place with a service of dedication at St. Paul's Cathedral on 3rd May 1951; the South Bank site opened daily from 4th May to 30th September 1951. With no room at this site for an amusement park, the Pleasure Gardens were located at Battersea. It was a nationwide festival with exhibitions held all over Britain. The official symbol was designed by Abram Games and shows Britannia on a rising star.

SOUTH BANK EXHIBITION, FESTIVAL OF BRITAIN 1951 AND HUNGERFORD BRIDGE, EMBANKMENT AND CLEOPATRA'S NEEDLE

The South Bank Festival site from across the Thames. The site was divided by Hungerford bridge into Upstream and Downstream areas connected by walkways beneath the bridge. The most visible buildings are, from the left: the shot tower, Royal Festival Hall (the only building intended to be permanent), the Dome of Discovery and the Skylon. 4½ acres of marshy land was reclaimed to build the new river wall and frontage. *(Published by Raphael Tuck, real photograph no. FB41.)*

This multiview shows some of the Exhibition halls, with a night view in the centre. The 300ft needle-thin Skylon dominates the scene; it symbolised a futuristic Britain, and was constructed of steel and aluminium to a design by Powell and Moya. By the end of the Festival about 9 million people had visited the Exhibition. *(Posted at the Exhibition in August, 1951; published by Raphael Tuck, real photograph no. FB36).*

THE DOME OF DISCOVERY, SOUTH BANK EXHIBITION FESTIVAL OF BRITAIN 1951

The Dome of Discovery, designed by Ralph Tubbs, caused quite a stir. At the time, it was the biggest dome ever built and housed exhibits on the Land, Sea, Sky, Outer Space, the Physical World and the Living World. In the right background, the roof of County Hall is visible. *(Published by Raphael Tuck, real photograph no. FB12).*

The transport pavilion had exhibits in several large halls, covering all aspects of the subject, such as navigation, signalling, telecommunication and design. There were also static exhibits outside – as seen here. On the left is the Regatta Restaurant, one of the twelve dotted around the site. *(Published by Valentine & Sons Ltd., real photograph no. V37).*

INTERIOR POWER AND PRODUCTION PAVILION   South Bank Exhibition   Festival of Britain 1951

Few postcards show the interiors of the pavilions – probably because they were not brightly lit. Visitors entered this pavilion on the left with exhibits of metals along the gallery. Passing (or not) the tea bar at the far end, the next exhibit was 'Research' in the right-hand gallery, before descending to the main exhibit below – 'Machines at Work' – all working examples of British engineering in industry. *(Published by Jarrold and Sons Ltd).*

MAIN VISTA SOUTH, FESTIVAL PLEASURE GARDENS, BATTERSEA. VG55

Battersea Park was chosen as the venue for the Pleasure Gardens and could be reached by shuttle buses or river boats from the main site. The well-known funfair was added for the Festival. While the Festival was open there were also exhibitions of open-air sculpture and "mobiles". There were refreshments kiosks at various points and girl orange-sellers dressed in Nell Gwynne style, to recall the days of Charles II's Vauxhall Gardens. *(The card was posted in Battersea in September 1951, by a visitor who had had a wonderful time at both South Bank and Battersea but "oh my feet"! Published by Valentine).*

"NEPTUNE" THE FAR TOTTERING AND OYSTERCREEK RAILWAY, FESTIVAL GARDENS, FESTIVAL OF BRITAIN 1951 EV 32

THE GUINNESS FESTIVAL CLOCK, SOUTHEND-ON-SEA

E.V.93—PROFESSOR SEPTIMUS URGE AT THE CONTROLS OF THE SHELL B-PLANE X-100, FESTIVAL PLEASURE GARDENS, BATTERSEA

One of the attractions at Battersea was the miniature railway designed by Rowland Emmett (1906-1990) – "The Far Tottering and Oystercreek Railway". Emmett specialised in elaborate and fanciful models and inventions, which is clearly demonstrated in this view of one of the engines – *"Neptune"*. The other engines were *"Nellie"* and *"Wild Goose"*. The railway caught everyone's imagination and received worldwide coverage, making Emmett famous. It carried visitors around the pleasure gardens, passing equally bizarre railway scenery with signs such as *"Do not tease the engines"*. *(Published by Valentine and posted in London in September 1951).*

Another Emmett creation – Professor Septimus Urge at the controls of the Shell BiPlane X-100 – one of the exhibits. *(Published by Valentine).*

Also in the Pleasure Gardens, the Guinness Clock was constructed as one of the "mobiles". According to the sign, the clock was designed from "a whimsey by Lewitt-Him" and constructed by The Franco British Electrical Co. Ltd. The clock had several moving parts, many of which have been triggered for this picture. Once the Festival was over, the clock toured the country and was erected in several tourist spots for a few weeks at a time. It is seen here at Southend-on-Sea, and was illuminated for the summer season. *(Posted in Southend, September, 1954; published by Raphael Tuck).*

FESTIVAL SHIP CAMPANIA, FESTIVAL OF BRITAIN 1951

The *Campania* housed a travelling exhibition, a smaller edition of the South Bank Story. The ship was moored at Southampton from 4th-14th May, before sailing to Dundee, Newcastle, Hull, Plymouth, Bristol, Cardiff, Belfast and Birkenhead, staying at each port of call for 10-14 days before the final visit to Glasgow where it remained from 18th September – 6th October. There was also a land-based travelling exhibit which visited Manchester, Leeds, Birmingham and Nottingham. Together, these mobile exhibitions provided a glimpse of the Festival for all parts of the country. This card was bought in Cardiff in August 1951. *(Published by Valentine).*

Events and Disasters

The period from 1900 until World War 1 was the "Golden Age" of the picture postcard. Photographers covered all manner of occasions, both large and small from celebrations to disasters. In later years newspapers provided pictures of this sort and postcards of events became few and far between. In the fifties, the Festival of Britain and the Coronation were very well covered by the postcard publishers but other events received scant attention.

The Coronation Stone was stolen from Westminster Abbey on Christmas Day, 1950. It was removed from its place beneath the Coronation Chair, where it had been for 650 years. The stone is a hefty slab of sandstone, weighing 458lbs, and had to be dragged to a waiting vehicle. Scottish nationalists claimed responsibility, saying that the stone was being returned to its rightful place as it had been taken from Scone in Scotland, in 1296, and England had promised to return it. The Stone was missing for 107 days, until found on 11th April 1951, abandoned at Arbroath Abbey; the thieves were never found. The police displayed the stone for the press, before it was transported back to London. *(Published by Valentine).*

In 1953, the American Ambassador, Hon. W.S. Gifford, and Admirals unveiled a plaque to John Paul Jones, Father of the American Navy. John Paul commanded a British merchant ship and added "Jones" to his name when he fled to Virginia in c.1773, to escape a murder charge. He fought for the colonists in the War of Independence. The plaque was fixed to the wall of the cottage where he was born, in 1747, at Kirkbean. The pictures on the card show the plaque, the Ambassador and Admirals, the cottage and the Paul Jones Hotel with the Southerness-on-Solway golf course behind. *(Published by Robert Dinwiddie & Co. Ltd.).*

The American-owned *Flying Enterprise* had left Hamburg on Christmas Day, 1951. Mountainous seas and hurricane winds damaged the vessel, so that on Boxing Day, Captain Henrik Carlsen ordered passengers and crew to abandon ship. The captain and a young ship's mate stayed on board in the hope that the freighter could be saved when conditions improved. However, the ship was soon listing at an 85-degree angle and its smokestack was clipping the top of the waves. They managed to secure a line from a British tug but the storms worsened and the exhausted pair realised that nothing more could be done. On 10th January, 1952, they leapt from the funnel and swam to safety. Just 40 minutes later the vessel slipped beneath the waves off Falmouth. The postcard shows the ship in its final hours; the arrow points to the captain and ship's mate, just before they abandoned ship. *(Posted in Amsterdam, January, 1952; published by Ampfoto).*

The World Scout Jubilee Jamboree was held on the rolling acres of Sutton Park, Sutton Coldfield, from 1st-12th August 1957. It celebrated fifty years of scouting and the centenary of Sir Robert Baden-Powell (1857-1941), who had fought at Mafeking and introduced some Zulu words to scouting. This meeting was described as an *"Indaba"* which is a Zulu word meaning an important tribal conference. *(Published by Valentine).*

AN OLD WORLD GARDEN by Granville Ellis.   244 "DAILY MAIL" IDEAL HOME EXHIBITION, 1958.

The 1958 "Daily Mail" Ideal Home Exhibition was its Golden Jubilee and was reported to be the most *"beautiful and impressive"* since being founded by Lord Northcliffe. Over 1,320,000 people and several members of the Royal Family visited the Jubilee Exhibition. The main feature was the Grand Hall, which was transformed into Parisian scenes such as the Palace of Fountainebleau and the Tuileries Gardens. Other features were the Women's Institute Market, Chivers Cookery Theatre, *"Woman"* fashion theatre, a very popular "Do-it-Yourself" section and gardens laid out by well-known British nurserymen. This is Granville Ellis's Olde World Garden set against a painted backdrop. The visitor who sent this card thought the gardens were beautiful *(Posted in Guildford, March 1958).*

On 15th August 1952, after hours of heavy rain, the East and West Lyn rivers burst their banks and rushed down towards Lynmouth carrying huge boulders, trees and tons of rubble. This monstrous "wall of water" crashed through the town to the sea, destroying everything in its path. In 12 hours 90 million tons of water devastated the village, leaving 34 people dead, 93 houses and buildings destroyed, 28 bridges demolished, 132 vehicles smashed beyond repair and 19 boats sunk; many birds and animals also perished. An emergency clear-up was started the next day and a nationwide appeal was launched for the flood victims. The steep gradient of Lynmouth Hill only added to the problems as the heavy bulldozers, cranes and

excavators had to edge down the hill in low gear, taking a considerable length of time to reach the stricken area. Of the 100,000 tons of rubble cleared from the riverbed, 40,000 tons were used to rebuild the sea-wall – a further 100,000 tons of debris was removed from the village streets. It took a month to finish the clearing up and to demolish the unsafe buildings. The card shows the scene on 16th August, looking towards the remains of the East Lyn bridge. The mound of rubble reaches to the top of the ground floor of the Lyndale Hotel. In the foreground, soldiers are erecting a temporary footbridge across the rushing water and debris. All the buildings here were eventually demolished. (Published by Harvey Barton & Son Ltd., of Bristol).

A photograph taken on 17th August, looking in the opposite direction. It shows the badly-damaged front of the Lyndale Hotel on the left and the still swollen waters of the West Lyn river which had divided and found a new course down this street. Several other damaged buildings are also visible. (Published by Harvey Barton).

Less than 6 months later, the country was devastated by another flood disaster, this time on the East coast. At the beginning of February, 1953, high tides and hurricane winds combined to cause severe damage from Lincolnshire to Kent. The surge of water smashed the sea defences and flooded large areas inland, so that thousands of people had to be evacuated. The heaviest loss of life was in Essex where most people were in bed when the tidal bore struck. A major rescue operation was mounted with servicemen struggling to repair and plug the gaps in the sea defences before the next high tide. Altogether, 40,000 people had to be evacuated – including the whole of Canvey Island. The final death toll was over 300 people. Over 30,000 were left homeless and the cost of flood damage was some £40 million. As well as Britain, the Netherlands also suffered widespread flooding when dykes burst, drowning over 1,000 people. The Lord Mayor's Flood Disaster Fund raised a significant sum which was shared between victims in both countries. For the affected resorts, the following weeks were a busy time, hastily rebuilding for the summer season. Being keen to attract visitors, it was thought undesirable to show the destruction the storm had wrought, so postcards were issued showing the newly-built parts; the aftermath of the storm is recorded on just a few postcards of Mablethorpe and Skegness. The close-up of the shelter at Mablethorpe shows how the promenade was completely destroyed, with "Greetings from Mablethorpe" on the reverse. No publisher indicated on either card.

A Postcard from the Fifties   13

Customs and Traditions

HELSTON FURRY DANCE

This annual event is held on 8th May at Helston, Cornwall. The day is given over to festivities but the principal dance is at noon and is headed by the Mayor, wearing his chain of office – he can just be seen in the picture on the bottom right. The men wear formal morning dress and the ladies wear their finest frocks. This card shows the long, full-skirted dresses that are typical of the early fifties. *(No publisher indicated).*

LONDON, CHRISTMAS TREE, TRAFALGAR SQUARE.

The postcard shows carol singers around the splendid Christmas Tree in Trafalgar Square. A giant tree is sent every year by the people of Norway for Britain's assistance during World War 2, when that country's king and government took refuge in Britain after their occupation by Germans. Inappropriately, this card was sent as a birthday card in September 1952. *(Published by C. Richter Ltd.)*

MISS ANN WRIGG "LADY GODIVA." 1951. COVENTRY
COVENTRY EVENING TELEGRAPH (PHOTO)

The crowd lining the streets of Coventry are wearing coats whilst Miss Ann Wrigg, as Lady Godiva, braves the cold on this chilly June day in 1951. The annual procession was to celebrate the legend of Lady Godiva and Peeping Tom. There is a statue and a clock showing both figures in the Broadgate Precinct. The card was sent in August 1951 by someone working on the rebuilding of the city after the extensive bomb damage suffered during World War 2. *(Published by the 'Coventry Evening Telegraph')*

London Life at the beginning of the decade – a group of costermongers parade through the streets of Southwark. They are called 'Pearlies' because their clothes are adorned with thousands of pearl buttons, sewn on in patterns. There has been a Pearly King of London since the Festival of Britain in 1951. The little girl on the left is dressed in typical early fifties clothes – a warm coat with a velvet collar, lace-up shoes and a big floppy bow in her hair. *(Published by Charles Skilton Ltd., London Life series no.1).*

1.   LONDON LIFE: Costermonger "Pearly Kings and Queens" in Southwark.   Photo: G.P.U.

Promotional cards

Postcards are sometimes used to advertise or promote an event. In the fifties, the postcard rate was cheaper than letter postage – and, of course, no envelope is required.

Advance notice of Liberace's concerts is given on the front of this postcard which was sent to a member of his fan club by International Artists Ltd., of Hollywood and posted on 20th May 1959 – just in time to book seats for the concerts. Liberace was somewhat derided in the 1950s but retained a loyal following of fans of all ages. Adverse criticism of his act, in 1954, provoked his reply *"What you said hurt me very much. I cried all the way to the bank!"*

"Nana" is a character from the Walt Disney film *Peter Pan*, released in 1953. The postcard is French and one of a set given away with Tobler Chocolates during the 1950s. All the cards portray Disney characters and there was a free album in which to collect the cards. The reverse of the cards have adverts for other French Disney merchandise.

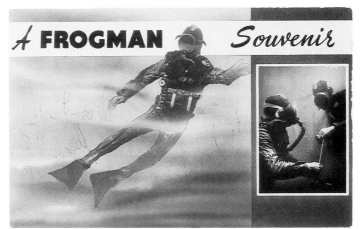

Land Rover issued some attractive coloured postcards to advertise their new Series II models in 1958. They are unsigned paintings, possibly by Terence Cuneo – who specialised in such subjects at the time. The first 4-wheel-drive vehicles appeared in 1949 and over the next 10 years had built up an unrivalled reputation with more than 200,000 in service world-wide. Series II models were supplied with either diesel or petrol engines, deeper and softer seats, easier bonnet opening and a choice of six attractive colours. The upmarket, Long Station Wagon is depicted at an airport and is in a shade of blue. The smaller 86" Wheelbase version is the more usual bronze-green colour. *(Posted from London in 1958, card no. 520).*

This postcard has been autographed by three people – R. Carswell, C. Richards, and Ian Fraser V.C., whose book *Frogman V.C.* was published in 1957. It tells of his exploits in the Royal Navy during World War 2, particularly his work in the Far East. He was awarded the Victoria Cross for a dangerous mission in Singapore, where he commanded the midget submarine that laid the mines and depth charges that severely damaged the Japanese cruiser *Takao*. It seems that this card was used to promote the book.

A new age of technology

The 1950s was a time of great technological achievement and Britain was a major force in the development of new ideas. Some examples are shown here whilst several others are illustrated or mentioned under the relevant subject heading.

DOUNREAY EXPERIMENTAL ATOMIC REACTOR ESTABLISHMENT, CAITHNESS   *Copyright—J. Adams*

The first planetarium opened in Munich in 1923. The first in Britain was the London Planetarium which opened on 19th March 1958 at Madame Tussaud's. The postcard shows the Chief Narrator explaining how the great Zeiss projector worked. The information on the back of the card describes it in detail – *"...weighs over 2 tons, projects images of the Sun, Moon, Planets and 9,000 stars. It can show the night sky as seen from any place on the Earth's surface for any time during the Past, Present, or Future"*. No wonder it cost £70,000! Despite the interesting show that should fascinate young and old alike, a contemporary guide book suggests that *"it is a handy place for a rest after walking round the waxworks!" (Published by the London Planetarium).*

The construction of the giant 250ft steerable telescope at Jodrell Bank began in 1952. It is situated in rural Cheshire just 20 miles from Manchester, at the site of the Nuffield Radio Astronomy Laboratories and is part of Manchester University. It was completed in 1957, and research started straight away. In May 1959, the telescope transmitted radio messages to the USA, via the moon. *(Published by Valentine).*

JODRELL BANK RADIO TELESCOPE, CHESHIRE.
Research into Radio Astronomy started in 1957. Total weight 2,000 tons. Diameter 250 ft. Height of rim in upper photograph approximately 300 ft. above ground level.

The U.K. Atomic Energy Establishment was set up in August 1954. Dounreay was the first fast breeder nuclear reactor, inaugurated on 14th November 1959. It was built as a research station; the reactor was fuelled by a mixture of plutonium and uranium oxides, and had its core immersed in a tank of liquid sodium. The photograph was taken as the workers were leaving through the gate on the left. *(Posted at DIngwall, September 1961; real photograph by John Adams).*

The hovercraft was the brainchild of Sir Christopher Cockerall, an electronics engineer, who patented the idea in December 1955. His early experiments were carried out using two empty tins and a vacuum cleaner, with the switch reversed to expel air. The picture shows the first full-size hovercraft – S.R.N.I., – built by Saunders-Roe and launched at Cowes on 30th May 1959. The first channel crossing was made on 25th July 1959 and the picture shows the landing at Dover with lots of curious holidaymakers watching. *(Published by Valentine. The card was not posted until June 1961).* Card from Ken Pemberton collection.

Comic cards that mirrored life

"Oscar the Pup"

WOT A LIFE!" SAYS OSCAR!

This series of comic cards is a little different from the 'saucy' cards usually associated with the Bamforth company. The first series of cards showing the antics of the delightful "Oscar the Pup" was drawn by Douglas Tempest. After his death in 1954, the series was continued by Brian Fitzpatrick. The pictures frequently illustrate new ideas and inventions of the 1950s - and Oscar's thoughts on such things. All the cards were published by Bamforth & Co. Ltd., and drawn by Brian Fitzpatrick, except for this one. This is one of the first cards, drawn by Doug Tempest, showing a new 'Zebra' crossing. *(Posted in Llandudno, September 1955; no. G110).*

WELL, IT DOES SAY **HELP YOURSELF!**

Self-service was a new experience for shoppers - this drawing illustrates the true meaning of the words! In 1950, there were few such stores in Britain - Sainsbury's first self-service store was opened in Croydon in July 1950. As the number of self-service stores increased, shoppers were warned against overspending as 'helping yourself' seemed to encourage people to buy what was on offer instead of simply what they needed. *(No. G299).*

THEY NEVER SEEM TO PICK MY NUMBER! "Oscar the Pup"

The government announced the introduction of Premium Bonds in April 1956, when they were mocked by the opposition as a 'squalid raffle'. The first bonds were sold on 1st November and could be bought in units of £1. 'ERNIE' drew the first prizewinners on 1st June 1957, with a top prize of £1,000. *(No. G232).*

NOTICE PARKING METERS NOW IN USE

THANK GOODNESS LAMP POSTS ARE STILL FREE!

On 10th July 1958, 625 of the dreaded parking meters came into operation in Mayfair - and many motorists simply moved to the nearest unmetered street! The 6d charge was for an hour's parking. *(No. G252).*

GIVE YOUR DOG BOW WOW HE'LL LOVE IT!

I'VE ALWAYS TO MAKE DO WITH OLD FASHIONED BONES!

Television advertising began with the launch of an independent channel in September 1955. The first advertisement was for Gibbs S.R. Toothpaste. The slogans and jingles of those early commercial breaks soon became part of everyday life. *(No. G256).*

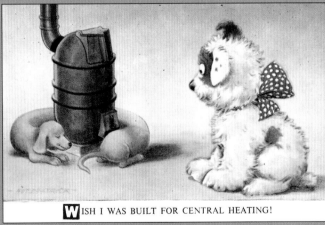

WISH I WAS BUILT FOR CENTRAL HEATING!

After the austerity of the immediate post-war years, people lavished time and money on their homes in the 1950s. They were encouraged to try 'do-it-yourself' decorating and maintenance, and many upgraded their homes, especially when supplies of furnishings and household appliances became cheaper and readily available. New homes were better designed and equipped. The open coal fires of the past were replaced by smokeless fuel-burning stoves or central heating. The extra warmth was appreciated by the whole family - including their pets! *(No. G300).*

Railways

In 1955, a modernisation plan was authorised by the government. This was intended to introduce diesel and electrification of the railway system, upgrade the freight business with new wagons and yards, and tackle reconstruction of the track to put right the cut-backs in maintenance that had been caused by the war. The following year, it was announced that the first line to be electrified would be Euston to Liverpool and Manchester. Also in 1956, the Motorail operation was inaugurated. For passengers, the third class coaches were abolished in 1956, leaving just two classes of travel. The changes did not take place quickly enough to prevent British Rail from making huge losses and forcing the closure of branch lines. Parish councils appealed for these to be kept open. In 1959, 230 stations faced closure and fares were raised by up to 50%.

A steam train approaches Dawlish from the west, whilst a goods train passes in the opposite direction – its steam can be seen against the cliff. In this decade, the steam locomotive was still a common sight. Many holidaymakers must have travelled to their destinations by train and for most it was an exciting start to their break. Ominously, a line of parked motor cars is also prominent. As these became available to more families, rail travel became less attractive. *(Published by Chapman & Sons, no.24123).*

DAWLISH from THE ROYAL HOTEL. 24123.

This was the way to travel to Paris in style. However, the Golden Arrow was not a boat train. From London to Dover or Folkestone, a British locomotive hauled the nine first-class Pullman coaches (it is just possible to make out the golden arrows on the bottom half of the coaches). Passengers then boarded a boat for the cross-channel stage and from Calais, a French locomotive completed the journey to Paris (called the 'Fleche d'Or'). The journey took 7½ hours, but passengers travelled in the lap of luxury as the Pullmans were superbly appointed with efficient, bi-lingual service. The card shows a train hauled by the Merchant Navy Class no.35028, *Clan Line*, passing a signal box at Petts Wood. *(Published by Valentine).*

THE GOLDEN ARROW.

THE HEART OF MIDLOTHIAN

By the end of the fifties, steam engines were gradually beginning to be replaced by diesel and electric. There were many factors to take into consideration – the rising price of suitable steam coal, the extra time steam engines needed for servicing and the shortage of trained footplate and maintenance staff. At the end of 1957, bulk orders were placed for new diesel locomotives of several types. This is an English Electric Class 4 Diesel Electric locomotive, no.D206, one of the first of this type, that were introduced in 1958. "The Heart of Midlothian" was a Scottish express, seen here approaching Offord and Buckden station, Huntingdon. (Posted in Heswall, October 1959; published by Valentine).

On the road

The post-war motoring boom really began on 26th May 1950 – the date that petrol rationing ended. The following weekend, Whitsun Bank Holiday, the volume of traffic was the highest yet seen. This was despite an increase in petrol tax imposed in the April budget, bringing the average price of a gallon to 3/- (15p). Car ownership enabled people to travel further afield to work, to shop and for holidays – so wider and better roads were called for and, at journey's end, somewhere to park. As more and more traffic poured into our towns and cities, it became obvious that some control was necessary and so, in 1958, parking meters were introduced. Yellow 'No Waiting' lines came into force. Roads themselves were improved: surfaces were strengthened, carriageways widened, bends straightened and junctions re-aligned. By 1956, 6,000 miles of new road had been laid since the war and plans were approved for a motorway system. Other improvements were the introduction of radar speed checks, and in built-up areas, sodium lighting. The race to keep motorists 'on the road' was a seemingly endless task!

Car parks are rarely the main subject of a postcard so this view of the 'New Car Park, Stranraer' is unusual. Visitors preferred to send scenic views; however, this line of contemporary cars will be more interesting to future generations than an unchanged landscape! Being a market town and seaport with a ferry service to Larne, more parking spaces would be required with the shift from public to private transport. There is one major difference to our car parks of today – most public car parks then offered free parking! (Published by Miller and Lang in their 'National Series').

The Talyllyn Railway Preservation Society was formed at a public meeting in Birmingham in October 1950 – the first such society in the country. It was decided to raise funds by public subscription and run the railway with volunteers. This narrow gauge line had opened in 1865 to link the slate quarries with the standard gauge line at Towyn. After the quarries closed in 1946, it continued to carry some passengers to local villages. In the 1950s, the line became well-known with the oft-repeated television film showing a journey from Towyn to Abergynolwyn. The card shows a queue for tickets at Towyn Wharf station and the engine *Edward Thomas* (ex Corris Railway) ready to haul the train. (Published by Talyllyn Railway, real photograph no. T.R.22).

The broad white bands of 'Zebra' Crossings were first painted on British roads in 1951. They made pedestrian crossings more noticeable to motorists and must have saved many lives since. The old glass, flashing belisha beacons had been used to mark crossing places since 1934 but were constantly being broken, so the glass was replaced by plastic globes from 1952 onwards. The new road layout and crossing are the prominent features on this view showing people crossing from the town, on the right, to the promenade, at Rhyl (Posted in Rhyl, August 1957; real photograph, no.G98A).

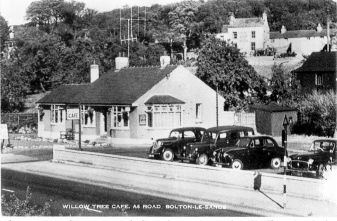

As more and more people bought cars to enjoy the 'freedom' of the road, families set off on long journeys to visit relatives, places of interest or simply to go for a 'run' in their new vehicle. To cater for these travellers, roadside restaurants and cafes were opened, especially on the major trunk roads. This is the Willow Tree Café, situated on the busy A6 between Lancaster and the Lake District. It seems to be a converted bungalow with the side garden surfaced to make a car park. (no publisher indicated).

Start of the mass motoring age

By the mid-fifties, many families could afford to own and run a small saloon car - once considered a luxury item. Car design altered considerably as the years went by. In 1950, many models were simply updated versions of pre-war cars. As demand increased, designers working for major manufacturers produced a wider range of models in a variety of colours and sizes, from luxury limousines to tiny 'bubble' cars. Throughout the decade, instruments and mechanical features became more sophisticated. The first major improvement was the legalisation of flashing direction indicators - in place of hand signals and trafficators - on 1st January 1954. (The correct use of hand signals was to remain part of the driving test for many years to come). It was also suggested that roadworthiness tests on cars should be carried out on a regular basis, but the M.O.T. test was not introduced until 1960. All the postcards on these two pages were issued by the manufacturers of the cars and were usually given away to potential customers. None of them has been postally used.

The Standard Eight first appeared in 1953 and was manufactured at the Coventry works. The slightly larger 'Ten' appeared a year later, and the two models were produced in various types until 1960. At its launch the saloon cost £481 and was a very basic car. It had sliding windows and access to the boot was from inside the car. Maximum speed was 66 mph and it was claimed to run 45 miles to the gallon. As the picture indicates, it was aimed at the family market and, with over 135,000 produced, was obviously a popular vehicle.

HERE'S FORD POPULAR MOTORING

POST CARD

Priced to beat the Credit Squeeze

Outstanding performance

Powerful, 1172 c.c. engine

Unrivalled Service facilities

Lowest priced car in Britain

A safe, genuine 4-seater saloon

Ready for YOU – NOW !

at

This most basic of family cars was designed and manufactured in Britain, and over 155,000 were made at Ford's Dagenham works between 1954-59. This design is an update of the 1949 Anglia and had only the most essential instruments. Hand signals were a necessity as there were no trafficators; there is a short, single windscreen wiper and only tiny headlamps. Top speed was just over 60 mph. The reverse of the card gives 7 'Popular' reasons for purchase - the launch price was £390 (including purchase tax) which made it the world's cheapest 4-cylinder car.

THE MORRIS COWLEY
BRITAIN'S FIRST FAMILY CAR IN PERFORMANCE, ROOMINESS AND STYLE

In 1951, Morris merged with Austin to become the British Motor Corporation, making it the biggest motor business in Britain. B.M.C. continued to make cars under the old names and this vehicle was manufactured at the Morris factory in Cowley from 1954-56. The statement on the back of the card claims full six-seater accommodation and a *"Quality First"* finish, but it was not as popular as the Morris Minor and Oxford ranges, and only 17,000 were produced.

THE WOLSELEY FOUR-FORTYFOUR
GRACEFULLY STYLED FOR YOUR MOTORING PLEASURE

Wolseley Motors - also based at Cowley - returned to car production after the war, during which they had concentrated their entire resources on armaments production. The cars were luxury versions of Morrises until 1952. After that, separate up-market designs were used, with the 4-44 being one of the first. It was advertised as having *"fast car performance with small car economy"*. All Wolseley cars were protected against rust at a special plant installed at Cowley, and run on a conveyor system, with the car being treated with various processes, including immersion in a tank of 'Bonderite'. Almost 30,000 of the 4-44s were made between 1952 and 1956.

Mercedes-Benz "300 S"

THE M.G. SERIES MGA—PROFILED FOR PERFORMANCE

A much lower production figure - 760 - is given for this luxurious 2-seater cabriolet. It was produced by Daimler-Benz, *"the world's oldest automobile manufacturer"*, from 1952 to 1958 - a far cry from the basic, economical designs of the pre-war years. The postcard is from a set issued by the company in 1955. All were painted by the same artist and show various models from the firm's beginnings to the 1950s.

In the 1950s, this name was synonymous with the sports car. On 22nd September 1955, MG cars unveiled its new sports model - the M.G.A - a two-seater model that, with its 1956 coupé version, was produced until 1959, by which time a total of 58,000 had been sold. It had an entirely new chassis and streamlined body that was designed to appeal to sports car fans the world over.

THE RILEY PATHFINDER "FOR MAGNIFICENT MOTORING"

WOLSELEY 6-99

Some 5,000 Pathfinders were produced between 1953 and 1957 at the Abingdon works. The reverse of the card bears the advertising note *"Exhilarating, satisfying motoring awaits you at the wheel of the Riley Pathfinder. For power, road holding and elegance, the Pathfinder is outstanding even by Riley standards"*. The chromium strip along the base edge of the sides is clearly visible in this view. The firm became part of B.M.C. in 1962 - the final Riley rolled off the production line in 1969.

Towards the end of the decade, many cars were produced in two-tone colours. This elegant Wolseley was designed to appeal to *"those who appreciate the many individual refinements offered in these fine cars - at a surprisingly moderate outlay, too"*. It was only manufactured between 1959 and 1961 with a total of 13,108 vehicles produced.

Alec Issigonis is credited with creating economy motoring - first with his design for the Morris Minor in 1948 and then with the Mini Minor in 1959. This revolutionary car was produced in both Austin and Morris versions and has a very practical design, with the small wheels placed at each 'corner'. When launched in August 1959, the car cost £535. Just two weeks later, production was hit by an unofficial strike at B.M.C. Despite this, the car went on to be an outstanding worldwide success, appearing in numerous styles and types.

On the road

On very long journeys – and without the direct routes provided by our present motorway system, an overnight stop was often essential. Accommodation for motorists, situated on major routes, was the solution. According to the information on the reverse of this postcard, showing the Hotel Cottages, Boroughbridge, this place was *"The first Motel in Europe. Situated close to the new A1 Bypass, Yorkshire, England"*. A 1958 guide states that it had 16 bedrooms, all with bathroom, and charged from 38/- per day. In the licensed restaurant, breakfast was 6/-, lunch 10/6 and dinner 11/6.

In 1955, a major road improvement plan was announced. This expensive undertaking would provide a new motorway system and bypasses for several towns and cities. The first stretch of British motorway served both purposes as an 8.5 mile section of the M6, bypassing Preston. It was opened by the Prime Minister, Harold MacMillan, on 12th December 1958. Just over a month later, it had to be closed as frost had damaged its asphalt surface. The first section of the M1, from north of London to the Midlands, near Rugby, was opened on Monday 2nd November 1959. People flocked to see this new concept in motoring and on Sunday 8th November, the approach routes were lined by sightseers enjoying a picnic! The central reservation was a simple stretch of grass with signs and the 'hard' shoulders were also grass; lorries would sink into it! Two service areas opened - at Watford Gap in November and Newport Pagnell (seen here) in December. Their restaurants opened in 1960.

The "Ace of Clubs" at Lewdown not only served as a restaurant and hotel but also offered motorists the chance to re-fuel their vehicles! Situated on the busy A30 route to Cornwall, it was large enough to cater for coach parties as well. The building appears to be a converted row of cottages. Many enterprising people set up filling stations along our trunk roads, often using their houses as an office and erecting the petrol pumps on their re-surfaced front gardens. The purpose-built petrol station was not so common as today, and self-service was unheard-of. *(Published by Overland Views)*.

THE LOWER HALF OF VAUXHALL CAR-BODIES IS DIPPED IN A BATH OF PRIMER PAINT THAT FLOWS INTO EVERY CORNER OF THE BODY STRUCTURE. AFTER THIS, EIGHT SEPARATE COATS OF PAINT ARE APPLIED.

These cars are being dipped in the paint shop at Vauxhall's factory in Luton. The date is probably 1955, so this would be the chassis of the Wyvern, Velox or Cresta. The company moved to Luton in 1905, and General Motors took control of it in 1926. In the post-war years, all the motor companies were very busy coping with the demand for family cars.

How much are postcards worth? The vast majority of postcards published in the fifties - seaside comics and tourist views - are worth virtually nothing, because of their easy availability, lack of appeal to collectors, and the fact that many countryside and village views have changed little. Royalty cards are very common, having been published in huge quantities. The Festival of Britain was promoted heavily on postcards, particularly from Tuck and Valentine, though some cards by smaller publishers can be worth several pounds. There is immense interest in collectables of the Festival, with two specialist societies catering for enthusiasts. Ephemeral images, for example for TV or comic characters, are avidly sought by collectors, and *Dan Dare* or early *Thomas the Tank Engine* cards can sell for around £8. But it is in the area of change that collectors congregate, and street scenes of the Fifties are beginning to be recognised for the prized items that they are. Town postcard views of this era are generally acknowledged to be scarcer than postcards from the 1900-14 period, and their value is rising accordingly, with £2- £5 being a current going rate for street scenes oozing transport and pedestrian activity.

In the Air

FLY BEA IN EUROPE'S FINEST AIR FLEET

In 1946, part of our national airline, BOAC, was split so that British European Airways would serve Europe whilst BOAC concentrated on intercontinental travel. BEA soon established a network to the major cities of Europe and made substantial profits during the 1950s, becoming the leading European airline. The 1956 fares included flights from London to Paris for £10 and to Milan for £27. The plane shown in the top picture of this advertising card is the *Elizabethan* Class Airspeed Ambassador which could carry 47 passengers in its unusually roomy cabin – apparently the high wings afforded a good view of the scenery! The bottom picture is of a Vickers Viscount *Discovery* Class – one of the first to enter service in 1953. The Viscount was the world's first turbo-prop plane and was a huge commercial success, being bought by many foreign airlines. *(Posted at Wokingham, June 1955).*

People who used to travel by air before the war noticed a marked difference in the service offered in the 1950s. Airlines were now catering for the millions who wished to fly – on business or holiday – instead of the select few who were able to afford the luxury service of the 1930s. Pressurised cabins meant that planes could fly higher, so were more economic – unfortunately, on long journeys, this often meant their passengers suffered from "jet-lag". The biggest change was the introduction of jet aircraft on major routes, which were fast and could fly higher than older models. Cabin service changed too; stewardesses no longer had to be trained nurses – knowledge of first aid was sufficient. However, they did have to learn to serve full meals and drinks during a flight; before the war, meals were usually served on the ground during stopovers. Tourist Class services were introduced from 1951 onwards. All the cards on this page were issued by the airline concerned, for their passengers to use.

B.O.A.C. Jet-Prop Britannia 312

The Britannia was originally designed to carry heavy loads for long distances, at high speed and low cost. The 312 version was used by BOAC to inaugurate the first transatlantic passenger service by a turbo-prop airliner on 19th December 1957. The following year, using two Comet 4 planes, the airline made the first turbo jet-powered, transatlantic passenger crossings – one in each direction. The New York to London flight set a new transatlantic record of 6 hours, 11 minutes. *(Posted in New York, August 1958).*

"DAKOTA"   AIR KRUISE LTD.

A smaller, independent, British airline, Air Kruise, was established in 1946 by Hugh Kennard at Lympne airfield, using light planes for pleasure trips. In 1953, the firm was acquired by British Aviation Services and began cross-channel flights from Ramsgate – retaining the original name – and eventually operating scheduled services to Europe. The Dakota aircraft was an all-time best-seller. It could carry 28 passengers but lacked a pressurised cabin. *(Posted in Worcester, August 1957).*

The German airline was suspended after the war and it was not until January 1953 that a new airline, *"Luftag"* was formed. The Western Allies handed over civil air traffic control in West Germany to their federal government in July 1953. *Luftag* reverted to the name *Lufthansa* a year later, operated its first domestic service on 1st April 1955 and European services a month later. They used Corvair 340 planes (seen on this card) which could carry up to 44 passengers.

The American airline Transcontinental & Western Air changed its name to Trans World Airlines in 1950. It was operating worldwide and wanted a name that indicated its international status. The Super-G constellation was built by Lockheed and used by TWA for both domestic and international flights. On the bottom of this card, there is a reminder to passengers to *"Use your camera – remember your trip with pictures"*. The caption on the front is repeated in French on the reverse of the card.

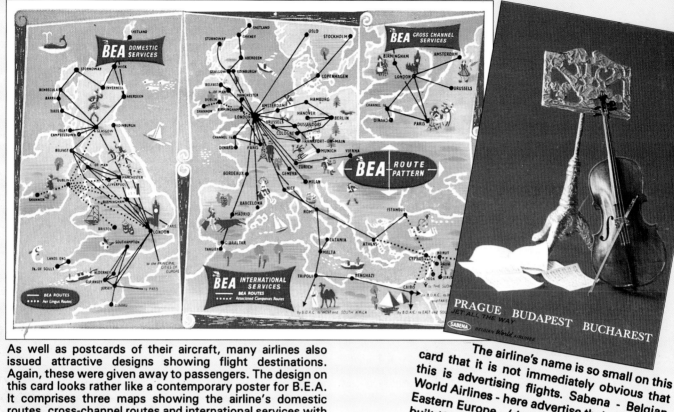

As well as postcards of their aircraft, many airlines also issued attractive designs showing flight destinations. Again, these were given away to passengers. The design on this card looks rather like a contemporary poster for B.E.A. It comprises three maps showing the airline's domestic routes, cross-channel routes and international services with onward travel by B.O.A.C.

The airline's name is so small on this card that it is not immediately obvious that this is advertising flights. Sabena - Belgian World Airlines - here advertise their service to Eastern Europe - 'Jet all the Way' - by French built 'Caravelle' planes.

This poster design for an Air France destination is signed by 'Nathan'. The reference on the back includes the date 1959, when Air France claimed to be *"The World's largest Airline'*.

T.W.A. issued many cards advertising their routes and services. This series of flight destinations has information on the location shown on the front - in this case it is repeated on the back in French.

In 1957 this Canadian airline issued a series of cards of artists' impressions of their European destinations. Here, a T.C.A. Super Constellation flies over Blarney Castle. On the back of the card there is a verse by John Locke, in English, and an enticing description of Ireland in French.

Airports

In the 1950s, long before stringent security measures were needed, spectators were well catered-for at airports and it was an exciting way to spend a day out. Coach-loads of visitors would converge on the new London Airport, just to watch the airlines at work – and to spot famous people as they passed through. Spectators had access to special viewing areas as well as the usual public areas of the terminal buildings. As the decade progressed, more people made use of air travel and airports were modernised to provide the extra space and facilities needed. In 1953, the world's airlines carried over 50 million passengers.

The old Great West Aerodrome was used by the R.A.F. during the war. Reconstruction of the civil airport began in 1944 and development of the site carried on apace from 1946 onwards. London (Heathrow) Airport Central became fully operational in April 1955. However, it soon became obvious that it would be unable to cope with the huge increase in air traffic, and a further £17 million expansion scheme was announced in 1957. This multiview, published in 1955, shows planes outside the South East Face Passenger building, central area from the air, the Control Tower, Main Passenger Concourse and the statue of the British aviators Alcock and Brown – who made the first non-stop transatlantic flight in 1919. *(Published by A.V. Fry & Co. Ltd).*

It took just seven months to build Lydd airport in 1954. It was built specially for Silver City Airways, who operated cross-channel car ferry services – hence the airport's name – Ferryfield. Silver City had inaugurated the service at Lympne airfield, on 14th July 1948. The first flight from Lydd was to Le Touquet in July, 1954. The cost of the 20-minute crossing was £27 for a car and 4 passengers. It was cheap, fast and became extremely popular; by the summer of 1955, over 35,000 vehicles and 88,000 passengers had used the service, and Deauville and Ostend were added to the destinations. This view shows several cars parked by the terminal, waiting to be driven onto a plane. In the fifties, this was the best way to start a European holiday; gradually, though, the new roll-on, roll-off boats offered a cheaper service and could carry a much greater number of vehicles. The airline became part of British United Ferries in 1963. *(published by Shoesmith & Etheridge Ltd).*

Spectators on the roof at London Airport in 1955 *(published by A.V. Fry).*

Ronaldsway airport, seven miles south of Douglas on the Isle of Man, was used by the RAF during the war and reverted to civilian use in 1946. BEA took over the bulk of passenger services in 1947 but it was also used by many independent airlines. The multiview shows the control tower in the centre with views of a plane landing, service in an aeroplane, De Havilland Rapides (owned by Manx Air Charters) and the airport from the air. The view of the cabin shows a rather cramped seating arrangement – however, the steward is serving drinks on a silver tray! The card was posted in Belfast, in August 1953, by a passenger who was flying for the first time and much preferred it to the boat. Their plane had stopped at Ronaldsway for 30 minutes en route to Belfast. *(Published by Photonia series.)*

Cars being unloaded from a Silver City freighter at Lydd. The card was posted at Dover in September 1954 with the message *"Just off on this..."* The aircraft was a Bristol Freighter which could carry 3 cars, 20 passengers; cycles and motor-cycles – as can be seen in the picture, all lined up for the photographer! The vehicles were driven on to the plane by airline staff using a set of wheeled ramps.

The decade was marked by several significant advances in aircraft development; e.g. the first supersonic fighter, swept-wing jet fighters, delta-wing aircraft, jet bombers and VTOL aircraft. Many civilian planes were developed from earlier military prototypes, and jet airliners were increasingly used on intercontinental routes as the years went by.

B.O.A.C. STRATOCRUISER IN FLIGHT.   LA.24

AVRO VULCAN

This luxury Boeing airliner was the civil counterpart of a military plane, the B50 atom-bomber. It was developed to meet the need for long-range airliners and, in the early 1950s, was the flagship of major airlines on their transatlantic and trans-Pacific routes. The planes had two decks, with the main accommodation on the upper deck and a spiral staircase descending to a lounge and bar on the lower deck. It was staffed by a crew of 10 and carried up to 100 passengers. The military version had a radome "chin" and the transport version – the Stratofreighter – was used at USAF bases in Britain. *(Published by A.V. Fry & Co).*

There were three "V" bombers – the Vickers Valiant, Handley-Page Victor and Avro Vulcan. The first was the Valiant with the prototype making its first flight in May 1951. The Vulcan was next in August 1952, with the Victor in December 1952. This picture shows the prototype Vulcan B.1, no VX770, the world's first delta-wing bomber, with a span of nearly 100ft. It was most impressive in flight and, despite its size, was very manoeuverable. With modifications, it went into service with the RAF in February 1957, as a long-range medium bomber. *(Published by Raphael Tuck).*

ENGLISH ELECTRIC COS CANBERRA B.I. Four Avon (Rolls Royce) R.A.3.
Max speed in excess of 600 m.p.h.

HAWKER HUNTER F.MK.I. Rolls Royce Avon Engine. Span 33ft. 7ins. Length 45ft. 9ins. Max speed in excess of mach 1.0
Armament 4 x 30 m m Cannon.

The Canberra was the first British-built jet bomber. In February 1951, the Mk2 was the first jet aircraft to cross the North Atlantic non-stop. The following year, it broke all records with a transatlantic round trip in a single day, taking just 7 hours 59 minutes. In 1953, a Canberra set a new world altitude record. An RAF Canberra photographic reconnaissance plane won an England to New Zealand air race in less than 24 hours. A true record-breaker! *(Published by J. Salmon Ltd., no.5269).*

The Hawker Hunter made its maiden flight in July 1951. In the fifties it was considered to be one of the best fighters in the world. Piloted by Sqn. Ldr. Neville Duke, Hawker's Chief Test Pilot, a Mk.3 Hunter established a new world speed record of 727.48 m.p.h., in September 1953. In those days, test pilots were celebrities and revered by schoolboys in the same way as sporting heroes. *(Published by J. Salmon Ltd. no.5270).*

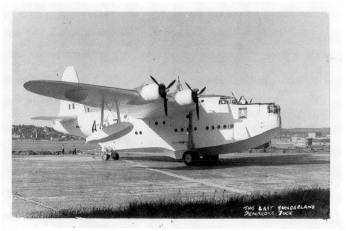

THE LAST SUNDERLAND PEMBROKE DOCK

As military planes became more sophisticated, older models had to be retired. The Short Sunderland flying boat was one of the RAF's longest serving operational aircraft. During World War 2, it was used on anti-submarine patrols and for maritime reconnaissance. The Luftwaffe called it the "flying porcupine" because it could defend itself so well from attacking enemy fighters. The final operational flight (and the last use of water-based aircraft by the RAF) was made on 15th May 1959. The aircraft was retired shortly afterwards and is shown here at Pembroke Dock. *(Published by Squibbs' Studios).*

Shipping

As the decade began, Atlantic passenger ships were having their most successful period ever. The liners, newly-refurbished after wartime service, were often full. These halcyon days were short-lived; the frequency and speed of the jet airliners soon displaced the ships as the most convenient method of intercontinental travel. Between Britain and Europe, the traditional cross-channel packet boats were joined by the new drive-on, drive-off car ferries.

Cunard RMS Franconia

During World War 2, the *Franconia* had been requisitioned by the British government for wartime service, which included serving as the British HQ during the Yalta conference of 1945. She was handed back to Cunard in 1947 and, after renovation, returned to the Liverpool, Quebec and Montreal service in 1949. The next year was an unhappy one for the liner. On one voyage, she went aground off Orleans Island, near Quebec City. On another occasion, after docking at Liverpool, she was found to be "stuffed with nylons" with a black market value of £80,000. Special customs investigators had boarded the liner and found the nylons tucked behind the ship's hull and hidden in first-class cabins. This 33-year-old ship was sold in 1956 and sailed to Inverkeithing, where she was broken up for scrap. *(illustration by Kenneth Shoesmith; card published by Cunard - ref. B683).*

R.M.S. "QUEEN ELIZABETH" LEAVES SOUTHAMPTON

The *Queen Elizabeth* was not completed until after the outbreak of World War 2, so was immediately put into service as a troopship. She was released from war service in 1946 and restored. With her sister ship *Queen Mary*, she was constantly in the news because of the number of celebrities who crossed the Atlantic on her. Before changing their allegiance to the *United States*, the Duke and Duchess of Windsor were frequent passengers. By 1958, when jet airliners had reduced travelling time from a leisurely six days to a few hours, the passenger numbers declined dramatically so that, by the end of the 1950s, 1.5 million people crossed the Atlantic by air and just 882,000 by sea. The postcard shows the liner departing with the help of tugs – the *Wellington* is in the foreground. *(Posted in Southampton, June 1956).*

SOUTHAMPTON.
OCEAN TERMINAL SHOWING R.M.S. QUEEN ELIZABETH

The stern of the *Queen Elizabeth*, at berth between voyages to New York, is seen here at Southampton's Ocean Terminal. The town's position at the head of Southampton Water had helped it become a chief British seaport and a terminal for most transatlantic shipping lines. The Ocean Terminal was opened in 1950 to cope with the huge number of passengers for sailings to all corners of the world. In the picture, spectators are standing on the second floor balcony watching the activity in this very busy port. There is an interesting variety of contemporary cars in the car park. The building was replaced, in 1983, by parking for imported cars. *(Published by Mason's Alpha series, real photograph, no.STN6).*

The Blue Riband of the Atlantic was won by the new American liner *United States* on 7th July 1952. The crossing from New York to Le Havre, her maiden voyage, had taken 3 days 10 hours and 40 minutes, at an average speed of 35.59 knots per hour. This beat the *Queen Mary's* record, set in 1938, by 10 hours. The *United States'* return journey took slightly longer – 3 days 12 hours 12 minutes. This United States Lines flagship was smaller but faster than Cunard's "Queens", but was still the largest liner built in the USA at that time. The cost of construction was offset by a contribution of £15 million from the US government, as the ship had a dual purpose – in times of war she could carry 1,400 troops. Work began in 1949 and she was launched in 1951; length 990ft, gross tonnage 53,350. She could take some 1,900 passengers and, for the rest of the decade, carried a full load including large numbers of American servicemen – in both directions. The Duke and Duchess of Windsor were regular passengers, as were members of European royal families and American politicians. *(Published by J. Arthur Dixon Ltd., no.SS.2).*

Norwegian Fishing Boats at Scalloway, Shetland   PN4627

Scalloway is the former capital of Shetland and is a busy fishing port. The harbour is usually full of fishing boats – the three larger boats here are Norwegian, whilst the one on the far side is the *Golden Harvest*. A dispute with Britain arose when Norway decided to extend her territorial waters for fishing purposes. It was settled in favour of Norway by the Hague International Court, in 1951. The final years of the decade again saw Britain involved in a fishery dispute but that time it was with Iceland – the so called 'cod wars'.

BRITISH RAILWAYS s.s. "LORD WARDEN"   6047.

British Railways' ship *Lord Warden* was the first purpose-built drive-on, drive-off Channel car ferry. It operated on the Dover to Boulogne route, with its first sailing on 17th June 1952. The opportunity to take a car to the continent so easily proved very popular with the rising number of private motorists. The card was sent by a passenger on this ship in August, 1955. (Published by Skyfotos).

The Shell Tanker *Zaphon* was built by Swan Hunter and Wigham Richardson Ltd., at Wallsend, and completed in 1957. For the time she was significantly larger than the average tanker, with a gross registered tonnage of 24,800 and a length of 700 ft. Orders for these larger tankers had been necessitated by the blocking of the Suez Canal in 1956 – the longer voyage round Africa made smaller vessels uneconomical. There was also an extra demand for oil for industry, power stations and of course, for transport.

SHELL TANKER s.s. "ZAPHON" 38.390 D.W. TONS.

The *Royal Iris* was a Mersey ferry and pleasure cruiser that sailed regularly from New Brighton and Liverpool on 'Dance Cruises'. She was built in 1951 for Wallasey Corporation as a dual purpose cruise/ferry vessel. In later years, she was used purely for cruising. In the centre of the card, the picture shows the boat on the River Mersey; the bottom views show the Bridge and Engine Room and the top views are of the ballroom and 'Fish & Chip Saloon'. The card was purchased on the boat in 1952, but was not posted.

IPSWICH, THE DOCKS.   V3985

A TIGHT FIT AT PORT ISAAC.

THE WOLF LIGHTHOUSE, LAND'S END   105

It was during the Industrial Revolution that Ipswich became a major port. This view of the docks shows the large mills and warehouses belonging to Cranfield Bros. The vessel in the foreground also belonged to the firm; it is the *Orinoco,* an auxiliary sailing barge, built in 1895, that had since been fitted with an engine and wheelhouse. *(Posted in Ipswich, August 1959; published by Photochrom, real photograph no. V3985).*

The dedication and bravery of the volunteer crews who man the British lifeboats have been responsible for saving thousands of lives since the RNLI was founded in 1824. Cornwall has several lifeboats based around its coastline. There was once one at Port Isaac which, astonishingly, was housed halfway up the steep, narrow village street and had to be brought down on wheels to be launched! As the caption on this card states, it was *"A Tight Fit at Port Isaac"!* It took many men to haul the boat back after a launch. The lifeboat was later replaced by an inshore boat, housed on the foreshore. *(Published by Lansdowne).*

For centuries, sailors have appreciated the dedication of the men who looked after the lighthouses around Britain's rock-strewn coastline. This light was built on Wolf Rock between 1862-69 and is 116ft high. It is situated 8 miles off Land's End. The postcard shows a small boat, on the left, and people on the rock – probably the arrival of supplies and a new shift of keepers. *(Posted in Penzance, July 1955).*

DOCK, HULL

This late 1950s view of King George Dock, Hull, has many ships moored at the piers. On the left are two local barges, the *Good Luck* and *Selby Robin.* The ports were still handling cargo using old, traditional methods – the container ship would soon alter working practices dramatically. Hull was badly affected by the strikes of 1955, when there was a dispute between dockworkers' unions. By August, over 12,000 dockers were on strike in London, Liverpool and Hull. Britain's shipping industry received a further blow with a strike of seamen at the same time. As the railways were also at a standstill owing to a strike by locomen, the Government declared a state of emergency; with similar problems in other industries it was a year of chaos for Britain. *(Posted in Bridlington, July 1960; published by Valentine & Sons Ltd., real photograph no.L9222).*

MAYFLOWER II   BUILT AT BRIXHAM
                                       by J. W. & A. UPHAM

A full size replica of *Mayflower* was built and sent as a goodwill gift to the citizens of the USA from the British people. The vessel, *Mayflower II,* was built at Brixham by J.W. & A. Upham and launched in 1956. It was sailed across the Atlantic in 1957 to Plymouth, Massachusetts, where it is moored as a permanent reminder of the original voyage by the Pilgrim Fathers in 1620. *(Published by Nicholas Horne).*

Holidays

In 1950, the first air charter holiday company was formed – Horizon of London. Foreign holidays were then an option for everyone and cheaper flights meant that even short holidays abroad were feasible. "Package" holidays were devised to cater for the British who had limited allowances of foreign currency and so the low prices in Spain were a big attraction. Coach tours were popular, but many people returned exhausted after rushing round from place to place trying to see everything in one visit!

This is Cala Mayor, in Palma, Majorca. Although some of the buildings have survived they are dwarfed by the new hotels that were built to cope with increasing numbers of foreign visitors to the island. By the end of the decade, the "package" holiday was a popular choice and over 3 million Britons holidayed abroad each year. *(Posted in Palma, 1955).*

This view of a tree-lined beach with just a few single-storey buildings is of Torremolinos, Spain. High-rise hotels and apartment blocks have changed the vista so that it is hardly recognisable today. The card was posted by a British holidaymaker on a day trip to Gibraltar, in June 1959. *(Published by La Galeria).*

This postcard shows Benidorm before the tourist onslaught with just a few buildings visible on its magnificent sandy bay. Benidorm became a tourist resort during the fifties. Bed and breakfast cost 110 pesetas per head (just under £1). The Germans built one of the first new hotels, on the hill above the village – as it was then. (Published by Edicaise Juquemo).

The British tourist industry was keen to increase the number of incoming visitors. Most of our holiday visitors came from the U.S.A., with the French and Germans the most frequent from Europe. It seems that a Convention of Travel Associations was held in Britain, in 1953. The enterprising Welsh Tourist Board sent postcards to delegates, hoping to influence them to promote holidays in Wales. The front and back of one of their cards is illustrated here. It was posted in London, in August 1953 and sent to California.

Wales—Fisherman with Coracle

British Travel Association Photograph

There is a postcard for each day of the week on this tour. Visitors were based at the *"Royal Hotel"*, Whitehead, Co. Antrim. The tour started on a Saturday, when they explored the attractions of Whitehead; Monday was the Giant's Causeway and Portrush; Tuesday was for shopping in Dublin and so on. This card is for Wednesday's tour of Belfast. When the itinerary was changed, the titles on the cards were altered accordingly. This card was posted in Whitehead in July 1953, sent by a young lady who was enjoying the tour but had had a rough crossing on the Irish Sea. *(Published by Devenny's).*

For more energetic people, a Youth Hosteling tour is an ideal holiday. Despite its title, the hostels are open to all ages. Patterdale is one of the Lakeland group of hostels, full details of which are given on this card. The hostel could sleep 25 males and 18 females, and had its own store. The simple map on the card shows the hostel's location but the relevant O.S. Map was recommended in the details on the front. The main ingredient for a happy hosteling holiday is good weather, the sender of this card was not so lucky – *"It was quite true about the weather, it's been raining all the time".* (Posted in Penrith, June 1953; published by Photocrafts Ltd.).

On the East coast, at Trusthorpe near Mablethorpe, were the Millfield Holiday Bungalows. These were semi-detached bungalows, with the office in the building flying the site flag, on the right. More expensive than a caravan, they did provide more room and privacy – almost a home from home. *(published by ARJAY Productions, real photograph no.90.272).*

Winkup's caravan site at Abergele *(posted at Rhyl in July 1954; published by Valentine).*

This multi-view and the previous card show the small, basic caravans that were typical of the 1950s. Most people arrived by public transport, and so there are few cars in evidence on either view. Both camps were close to the sea so, weather permitting, it was an ideal place for a holiday. Unlike modern caravan parks, there were few on-site amenities, and visitors travelled to the nearest resorts for entertainment. From Ulrome, it would have been Bridlington or Hornsea. *(Posted at Driffield in June 1955; published by The Northern Photographic Co.).*

At the seaside

803 A Summers Day at Polzeath

Although Britons could take advantage of the many overseas tours that were offered in the fifties, the traditional British seaside holiday was the choice for most families – if they could afford it. A good bed and breakfast establishment, a stretch of sand, some form of evening entertainment – and, hopefully, good weather – were the ingredients for a perfect week beside the sea.

A summer's day at Polzeath – having arrived at the seaside in the family car, the first priority was somewhere to park. As this view shows, it soon became crowded. It must have been a very hot day as some windscreens and radiators are draped with towels to keep them cool. There are all sorts of vehicles – vans, saloon cars, sports cars, convertibles – and they are parked so close together near the beach, that those in the middle would have been unable to leave until some of the others went home! *(Posted at Bodmin, September 1951).*

GY 22

GT. YARMOUTH. CENTRAL MARINE PARADE

By contrast, this picture of Great Yarmouth was taken on a dull day – but still the crowds have arrived. Perhaps it was a Bank Holiday, as there is hardly a parking space left. Few were brave enough to discard their coats, so it must have been chilly too. The Marina is on the right, with Britannia Pier in the distance. A placard in the right-hand corner advertises the *News Chronicle* and offers £5 to anyone who can spot their character "Lobby Lud" – a popular gimmick with many newspapers at the time. *(Published by Mason's Alpha series, real photograph no.GY22).*

MARGATE SANDS IN SUMMER

Having reached the beach and hired a deckchair, a good spot on the sands was chosen – but this view shows that only the "early birds" would be able to do so. The caption reads *"Margate Sands in Summer"* – but there is no sand left uncovered here! The resort caters for over 2 million visitors annually. *(Published by Lincoln Press Ltd. no.ME38).*

THE SANDS AND CHILDREN'S PLAYGROUND, BURNHAM-ON-SEA   A TUCK CARD

There is more space for a deckchair here! Burnham-on-Sea has a large sandy beach and there is plenty of room for sandcastles. The children's playground is in the centre with swingboats and a merry-go-round. The sender of this card writes that they were having *"lovely weather"* *(Posted in Shepton Mallet, August 1958; published by Raphael Tuck).*

The weather was *"not so good"* in North Wales in August 1956, when this card was sent. Another quiet resort, Penmaenmawr is situated "twixt mountain and sea". It has a fine wide promenade with rows of smart chalets backing onto the railway behind. These chalets are a boon when the weather is changeable and provide a storage area for buckets and spades, and picnics, and serve as a changing room for wriggling in and out of bathing costumes. *(Posted in Bangor, August 1956; published by Raphael Tuck).*

PNMA 44   THE PROMENADE, PENMAENMAWR   A TUCK CARD

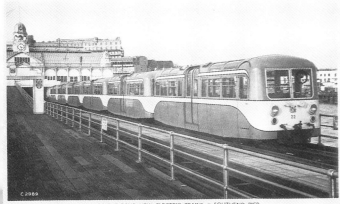

ONE OF THE FOUR NEW ELECTRIC TRAINS – SOUTHEND PIER

THE PIER AND PAVILION, COLWYN BAY

Mention "Southend" and most people immediately think of "The Pier" – and rightly so – stretching almost 1½ miles out to sea it is the longest in the world. Being the nearest resort to London, Southend became very popular with day-trippers. In 1888, it was decided to replace the old wooden jetty with this fine pier. It cost c.£60,000 and opened in 1890. The card is one of a set issued for the Diamond Jubilee of the pier in 1950 and shows one of the four new electric trains, ready for its journey to the seaward end of the pier. *(Published by Southend Corporation).*

As well as serving as a jetty, a seaside pier was a "promenade above the waves". Many piers boasted pavilions and offered a variety of entertainment. On Colwyn Bay pier, there were orchestral concerts and a "Summer Smiles" show as well as the usual slot machines. As this view shows, many people enjoyed strolling in the sunshine or simply relaxing in deckchairs.

COTMAN COLOR CARDS FOR CHILDREN   TWO'S COMPANY

DONKEY RIDES, WESTON-SUPER-MARE

Seated on a picnic hamper, with the family dog beside her, this little girl has all she needs for a perfect day on the beach – toy boats, a rubber ring, buckets and spade. The metal buckets were always brightly coloured and the one in the foreground has a picture of the liner *Queen Mary* on it. *(Posted in Lowestoft, June 1959; published by Jarrold & Sons Ltd., Children's series, "Two's Company").*

No visit to the beach would have been as exciting without a donkey ride. In the lengthening shadows, this team at Weston-Super-Mare look quite content and the people look tanned and relaxed – except for the young boy on the left, it was probably the end of a long day for him! *(Published by R.A. Postcards, London).*

A day at the seaside would not have been complete without a paddle in the sea; the "Belle of the Beach" is dipping her toe in the water as she poses on the left for the photographer.

The two "Belles" on the right are wearing bikinis which only became popular with the end of the hated clothing coupons and the subsequent renewed interest in fashion. First designed in 1946, this style of dress – or undress – was often frowned upon in the early 1950s. *(Published by Jarrold & Sons Ltd., Belles of the Beach series, nos. 5 & 9).*

A Postcard from the Fifties

Holiday Camps

After the war, holiday camps provided a value-for-money holiday for those who were not yet ready to venture abroad. The 1950s were the boom years for "campers". Five guineas paid for a week for one person's full board at a camp in 1950; this had risen to about £10 in 1959, or to £15 for one of the new self-catering chalets equipped with fridge and television. The biggest attraction of the camps was the "all-in" price – once through the gate, all the entertainment was free.

With so many exciting and different ways to spend the days, it's surprising that campers found time to purchase, write and send any postcards. This "lazygram" was published by Butlin's so that the writer could just tick the relevant comments and sign it – although there is still room on the back for a longer message. This card was printed for use at their chain of hotels at Cliftonville, near Margate, but there were probably versions for each of their camps. *(Butlin's Photographic Services Ltd.).*

Middleton Tower Holiday Camp

The Middleton Tower Camp was situated near Morecambe. Part of the complex was built to resemble an ocean liner and was called the *S.S. Berengaria* – the camp's motto was *"Cruising on Land"*. This multiview shows the tower with views of coaches lined up at the camp entrance; the reception area; the dining hall and the "Wonder Bar". The camp was later taken over by Pontins. *(Posted in Morecambe, July 1953; published by the camp).*

Middleton Tower Holiday Camp

Keeping the children occupied was never a problem. The message on this card explains *"...The children are thrilled with it and have been no trouble yet with something going on all the time for them to do."* As a result, they were usually so exhausted by bedtime that they were soon fast asleep, allowing their parents to enjoy the evening's entertainment. The young children here are queueing for a show in their own theatre which also served as a cinema. All the little girls have ribbons in their hair and many have the ringlets that were so popular at the time. *(Posted in Morecambe, June 1956; published by Middleton Tower Camp).*

As well as stage shows, evening entertainment usually included dancing to a live dance band. Some of these campers at Prestatyn Holiday Camp were obviously keen ballroom dancers as they had brought glamorous evening dresses to wear. What a contrast to the frenetic "disco" of today! *(Posted in Prestatyn, September 1958; real photograph by "Eric").*

PRESTATYN HOLIDAY CAMP

THE BALLROOM

"Butlin's – the holiday designed for the British climate" – claims a 1959 advertisement. There were six camps in 1950 – Ayr, Clacton, Filey, Pwllheli, Skegness, and Mosney in Eire. The other camps were not opened until the 1960s. The camps were always painted in bright colours as Billy Butlin believed that these were cheerful and meant that people were having a good time! Once a camper was signed in, there was no need to leave the camp as everything was provided and included in the cost of the holiday. Butlins cost a little more than other camps but claimed to be the best. Campers returned year after year for a holiday of few responsibilities with planned entertainment and guaranteed fun. Several well-known names in the world of show business started their professional careers at these camps – as redcoats.

THE CHALETS, BUTLIN'S HOLIDAY CAMP, SKEGNESS

BUTLIN'S
Redcoat operating Radio Butlin

A week in high season in the mid-fifties cost £9.25 per adult and £5.25 per child. The chalets were very basic as there was no self-catering then. This row of chalets is at Skegness, the first Butlin camp and had changed little since it opened in 1938. The card has the most uninteresting message ever sent; a camper writes *"I promised I would write again and I am fulfilling my promise by writing. I don't expect I will write again ..."*! Was she enjoying herself? We will never know! *(Posted in Skegness, August 1952; card no.10).*

On this postcard a redcoat operates Radio Butlin, but there is no indication of which camp she is at. In her right hand, the hammer is poised to make the "ding-dong" which preceded all announcements. If the clock was right, then it was not the *"Morning Campers"* or *"Wakey-Wakey"* that woke everyone in time for breakfast. The clock reads 3.15, so she was probably about to announce the start of a competition or show. The equipment is extremely bulky and she is faced with row upon row of dials and switches. *(Published by Butlin's, no.GV.11).*

A COMPETITION BY THE POOL   BUTLIN'S HOLIDAY CAMP, PWLLHELI

BUTLIN'S MOSNEY HOLIDAY VILLAGE, IRELAND   A DINING HALL

In the days before self-catering chalets, the whole camp had to be served their meals in dining halls – a mammoth task. At peak holiday times, this would be in two sittings. There must be hundreds of tables in this view, all with settings for eight people. In the centre, there are heated trolleys and serving stations from which the waiters would serve their allocated row of campers.

At Pwllheli, this is "A competition by the pool". There are only four girls left in the line-up so it must have been time to announce the winner. In the middle of the crowd, holding a microphone, is the celebrity Wynford Vaughan Thomas who was either judging the competition or presenting the prizes. There were lots of free-to-enter competitions during the week, covering all sorts of activities and talent. Prizewinners often returned for a final round at the end of the season. Major prizes were usually holidays for the following year. *(Posted in Pwllheli, August 1954; published by Jarrold & Sons Ltd.).*

A night out

Entertainment at the beginning of the decade was little different from what was on offer before World War 2. The cinema was very popular and there was no shortage of new films. Theatre, music and dance were well-patronised whether the production was by professional or amateur groups. By the end of the fifties, it was rather different. Many cinemas had closed; variety theatres and dance halls were used to cater for the new craze of Rock 'n' Roll and traditional theatre was eclipsed by a group of writers known as the "Angry Young Men".

BLACKPOOL TOWER CIRCUS.

If you were within reach of Blackpool, then a visit to the famous Tower Circus was a must. Charlie Cairoli (1910-80) is pictured here with his white-faced stooge, Jimmy Buchanan. They were masters of well-timed slapstick – Jimmy was on the receiving end of many a bucket of water. They were also fine musicians. Cairoli was the resident clown at this Circus from 1939 until the late 1970s, when ill-health forced him to retire.

Pineapple Poll (Scene 1)

Pineapple Poll was choreographed especially for the Sadlers Wells Ballet by John Cranko. It is based on W.S. Gilbert's *"The Bumboat Woman's Story"* and the music is from several of Sullivan's operettas, which were no longer under copyright. It opened on 13th March 1951, and starred Elaine Fifield as Poll, David Blair as Captain Belraye and David Poole as Jasper. The backcloth seen here was designed by Osbert Lancaster. *(Real photograph no.OV1).*

'THE DESERT SONG,' OPEN-AIR THEATRE, SCARBOROUGH 1952

The Open-Air Theatre in Scarborough was the venue for an annual summer musical which delighted residents and visitors alike. In 1952, it was *"The Desert Song"* which, according to the sender of this postcard, was *"...very good this year".* The picture shows the cast at the finale – the scenery is reflected in the water. *(Posted in Scarborough, July 1952).*

This water-colour drawing by the artist Bryan de Grineau shows a concert in progress at the Royal Festival Hall. Built as the only permanent feature of the Festival of Britain, in 1951, it was designed by Robert Matthew. Its auditorium has excellent acoustics and patrons enjoy a clear view of the platform from the projecting boxes. In its first year there were many concerts; the highlight of 1952 was a one-night concert by Boston Symphony Orchestra. *(Published by Royle Publications Ltd. no.P.C.17).*

At the beginning of the 1950s, Geraldo (1904-74) was the foremost dance band leader in Britain. His real name was Gerald Bright and, in the thirties, his music had earned him the nickname "Tango King". During World War 2, he was supervisor of the Band Division of E.N.S.A. In the 1950s, he was the music director of Scottish Television. Until the mid-1950s, dance bands were in great demand for the regular Saturday night dances which took place in most towns. Many band leaders became well-known celebrities, as they conducted their bands on live programmes on both radio and television, with *Come Dancing* being one of the BBC's most-watched programmes. The postcard has a facsimile signature on the front and on the back states *"Geraldo, one of the Stars who can be head on Philips – The Records of the Century".* *(Published by Celebrity Publishers Ltd., Celebrity Autograph series no.206).*

Streatham Hill Theatre opened in 1929. This photograph was taken c.1953, when the play being performed was *Ring Round the Moon,* translated by Christopher Fry from the original work by Jean Anouilh. The production starred Paul Schofield and Marie Lowe, who had transferred with the play after a very successful run of 682 performances at the Globe Theatre. The posters on the theatre advertise the next production which was to be *Pygmalion.* On the opposite corner, there is another common feature of fifties' towns – a milk bar. *(Posted in Streatham, August 1956; published by Frith & Co., real photograph no. STM30).*

London had its first new theatre for 300 years when the "Mermaid" opened in May 1959. It was the inspiration of Sir Bernard Miles and his wife, who set about raising funds from the City and public subscription to convert the shell of a blitzed Victorian warehouse alongside Puddle Dock, Blackfriars. It has no proscenium or orchestra pit, but the sloping auditorium gives a perfect view from all seats. *(Published by Gordon Fraser, real photograph no. LMMT-3).*

Danny Kaye (1913-87) scored an amazing success in Britain with his stage performances at "The Palladium" in 1948 and again, when he returned in 1949 for a long tour. He gave several performances in Britain in the fifties, as well as starring in films such as *White Christmas* and *Hans Christian Anderson* from which his songs *Thumbelina, The Ugly Duckling* and *Wonderful Copenhagen* proved to be perennial favourites on request programmes. He was presented with a Special Academy Award for "his unique talents and service to the American people" in 1954. *(Real photograph no.FS70, with no publisher indicated).*

This glamorous lady was a model before her singing talents were noticed She was soon much in demand to star in Britain's top night spots. Yana (1932-89), whose real name was Pamela Guard, soon secured a recording contract and had hit records including *Mr. Wonderful.* She starred in Rodgers & Hammerstein's *Cinderella* at the London Coliseum from which she had another hit with the song *Do I Love You,* a duet with Bruce Trent. In 1956 at the height of her popularity, she had her own BBC series and was a regular artiste on ITV's *Sunday Night at the London Palladium.* *(Published by Celebrity Publishers, Celebrity Autograph series no.353).*

A very unusual card of a restaurant in Knightsbridge, where the clientele are suitably dressed in tiara and evening clothes. This card was posted in London, S.W.1 by a customer who had eaten at the restaurant in April 1957.

A meal or a drink would complete the perfect night out. One possibility was Dirty Dick's Wine House in Bishopsgate, London. This postcard features views of the exterior, bars, cellar and buffet bar where fresh Whitstable oysters were 7/- per dozen. *(Published by View Card Issuing Co. Ltd., real photograph no. 2/A1872.)*

Cinema

"I'm still big. It's the pictures that got small". These words, spoken by the character Norma Desmond in the film version of Sunset Boulevard (1950), sum up the state of the cinema at that time. Few outstanding films had been made since the war and, in the USA, television was having a major impact on cinema attendances. The film industry had to fight back and did so with the introduction of new technology and some epic films. The first fifties epic was Quo Vadis (1951), followed by several others including The Robe (1953), The Ten Commandments (1956) and Ben Hur (1959). Most of these were filmed using a wide-screen technique, starting with The Robe which introduced CinemaScope in 1953. This was followed by other studio's big-screen systems such as VistaVision and Todd-AO. There was also the short-lived Cinerama and a brief craze for 3-D films. Improved sound systems and special effects enhanced all films from westerns to musicals. The younger generation enjoyed films starring the latest rock 'n' roll stars and the new teenage heartthrobs such as Tony Curtis and James Dean. To ensure that those under the age of 16 did not see "unsuitable" films, the British Board of Film Censors introduced the "X" certificate in 1951 – the first film to be awarded an "X" was a French one containing a sequence about artificial insemination. At the end of the decade, despite the closure of many cinemas, there was still an enthusiastic audience who looked forward to a night out "at the pictures".

For David Niven (1909-93), *Around the World in Eighty Days* (1956) proved to be his most successful film. He played the part of Phileas Fogg in this lavish costume adventure which was filmed in Todd-AO. He earned an Oscar for Best Actor and also received the New York Critics Award for Best Actor for his role in *Separate Tables* (1958). *(Published by Editions P.I., real photograph no.901A).*

Gregory Peck
Photo H.P.S.
Rock Hudson

By 1950, Gregory Peck was astute enough to command the sort of financial rewards that allowed him to choose only the roles he wanted to play. In the 1950s, he played leading roles in several films including *The Gunfighter* (1950), *Captain Horatio Hornblower* (1951), *Roman Holiday* (1953), *Moby Dick* (1956), *The Big Country* (1958) and *On the Beach* (1959). *(Published in Belgium, real photograph no. C7).*

By the mid-1950s, Rock Hudson (1925-85) was a top star and the decade was the most successful of his career. He was nominated for an Oscar for *Giant* (1956). During the fifties, his roles varied from westerns such as *Winchester 73* (1950) to comedies like *Pillow Talk* (1959). *(Published by Edition P.I., real photograph no.709A).*

This postcard shows Norman Wisdom in his first starring role in *Trouble in Store* in 1953, which provoked massive queues at British cinemas and was a box-office hit. In his trademark tight-fitting suit, he went on to star in many other British comedies, all filmed in black and white and all successful. At the same time, he continued with his stage and television career and, in 1954, had a hit song with *Don't Laugh at Me* which he co-wrote. Despite his tuneful plea, the British public *did* like to laugh at this seemingly vulnerable comedian. *(Published by L.D. Ltd., Film Star Autograph Portrait Series no.72).*

Although well-known as a child star, Elizabeth Taylor consolidated her position as a top box-office superstar in the 1950s. At the same time, her private life was also the subject of much press coverage. She was first married to Nicky Hilton when in her teens; in 1952, she married Michael Wilding and, in the late 1950s, Michael Todd. Her 1950s films include *Father of the Bride* (1950), *Quo Vadis* (1951), *Giant* (1956) and *Cat on a Hot Tin Roof* (1958). She was, of course, to go on to greater success – and more marriages – in the following years. The postcard shows her as she appeared in *The Girl who had Everything* (1953). (Published by L.D. Ltd., Film Star Autograph Portrait Series. no.131).

Marilyn Monroe (1926-62) had some small parts in films in the late 1940s but her first decent role was in *The Asphalt Jungle* in 1950. She went on to make several legendary films and became the world's most famous film star and sex symbol of the time. Among her best-known films were: *All About Eve* (1950), *Gentlemen Prefer Blondes* (1953), *The Seven Year Itch* (1955), *Bus Stop* (1956), *The Prince and the Showgirl* (1957) and *Some Like it Hot* (1959). Despite her success, her private life was not a happy one and she only made a couple of films in the 1960s, before her tragically early death at the age of 36. (Published by ISV, no.IV/6).

"The biggest new entertainment event of the year." - LIFE

Cinerama was launched in 1952. It was a process whereby films that had been shot on three cameras were projected by three projectors on to a wrap-around screen. This gave a very realistic image to the audience who could feel that they were actually taking part in the film. Stereo sound increased the sensation of "being there". One of the most realistic sequences of the original film *This Is Cinerama* was a roller-coaster ride – as seen on this postcard. Because it was a very expensive process to produce and project, it was only a passing craze and the film studios concentrated on the new big-screen systems instead. This coloured card shows an audience watching the roller-coaster ride; the reverse has the phrase *I was in Cinerama* and goes on to list the American movie theatres that would be showing the film. The card was sent to Milford-on-Sea, Hants, but is not dated. (Published by Shorecolour Co., New York).

The Davy Crockett stories were originally made for television in 1954/55 and shown as part of Disney's *Frontierland* series. They were later combined and issued for the cinema as *Davy Crockett* (1954) and *Davy Crockett and the River Pirates* (1955). The title role was played by Fess Parker, seen here. The theme song *The Ballad of Davy Crockett*, sung by Bill Hayes, was also a hit, reaching No.2 in the British music charts in February 1956. It seemed that all small boys knew of the "king of the wild frontier" and there was a great demand for replica coonskin hats! The reverse of the card has a paragraph of information on the real Davy Crockett (1786-1836). (Published by Valentine).

The music charts

In the early fifties, light music was "middle-aged" in style. Soon, however, teenage tastes were to transform the world of popular music. Coffee bars opened all over the country, where teenagers could drink "frothy coffee", served in glass cups from Italian Expresso machines, whilst listening to the latest records on a juke-box. As the old – and fragile – 78 r.p.m. records were replaced by 45 r.p.m. singles, and records became cheap and plentiful, the sales of records increased from £3$\frac{1}{2}$ million in 1950 to £15 million by the end of the decade. "Pop" music was here to stay. The first British list of top ten best-selling records appeared in the New Musical Express in November 1952, and contained mostly ballads. The first true published list appeared in Record Mirror on 22nd January 1955, and was increased to a Top Twenty on 8th October 1955. Ballads still dominated the charts but rock 'n' roll had begun to make an impact. "Six-Five Special", first televised in 1957, was a forerunner of "pop" music shows. It was hosted by Pete Murray and Josephine Douglas - with resident group Don Lang and his Frantic Five.

The film Rock Around the Clock was the cause of much concern amongst adults. Police were called to cinemas world-wide, to quell the "riots" and eject youths and "Teddy Boys" who were jiving in the aisles and letting off fireworks in the cinemas. They simply continued to jive, chant and clap on the streets; in Britain, many were fined for "insulting behaviour".

Lonnie Donegan was a great influence on the British music scene, as he popularised skiffle in this country. The Lonnie Donegan Skiffle Group had their first hit in 1956 with Rock Island Line, which reached No.8 in the charts during its 22-week run. They had a further 25 hit singles, 14 of them in the 1950s. Cumberland Gap and Puttin' on the Style both reached the No.1 spot in 1957, whilst later chart entries were Tom Dooley and Does your Chewing Gum lose its Flavour. The Group appeared regularly on BBC's Six-Five Special, (Published by Celebrity Publishers, Celebrity Autographed Series no.369).

GUY MITCHELL

With his song Feet Up, Guy Mitchell was at No.5 in the first British chart of 1952. He was very popular in the U.K. and had already had success with My Truly, Truly Fair in 1951. His other chart successes were She Wears Red Feathers (1953), Singing the Blues (3 weeks at No.1 in 1957) and Knee Deep in the Blues – both of which were covered by Tommy Steele – and, in 1959, Heartaches by the Number. (Published by Picturegoer Series, real photograph no. D303).

Bill Haley

Bill Haley (1925-81), the 30-year old with the kiss curl, started a new trend in pop music with his rock 'n' roll records. Shake, Rattle and Roll was listed at No.4 in the first Record Mirror chart of 1955. However, it was Rock Around the Clock that really stormed the charts, being No.1 for 7 weeks at the end of 1955 and remaining in the charts for 4 months. It was the theme from the film Blackboard Jungle. In October 1956, he had 5 titles in the British Top Twenty – Rockin' Through the Rye (no.5), Rock Around the Clock (no.10), Saints Rock and Roll (no.12), See You Later, Alligator (no.14) and Razzle Dazzle (no.14). This was the high point of his career but, from 1957, he could not compete with the younger stars who followed in his wake, and his later records failed to match his earlier success. (Published by Valentine, real photograph no. 39/2).

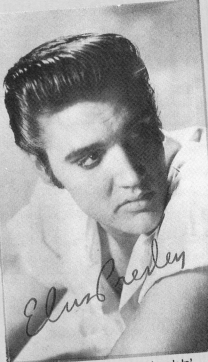

After Bill Haley introduced rock 'n' roll to the world, it was Elvis Presley (1935-77) who consolidated its appeal, especially to the teenage generation. With his style and sex appeal, he became the most influential performer of the decade. His first chart success was in 1956 with Heartbreak Hotel, which made him an international star. He had a further 20 British hit singles in the 1950s. (Published by D. Constance Ltd., no.321).

Tommy Steele was spotted singing rock 'n' roll in the Two I's coffee bar in Soho. He made his first record in 1956 – *Rock with the Cavemen* – which reached No.11 in the charts. His cover version of Guy Mitchell's *Singing the Blues* made no.1 in January 1957, with the original version topping the charts in the weeks before and after! In the fifties, it was quite common for artists to compete for a place in the charts with the same song – released at the same time! Steele's other well-known fifties hits include *Butterflies, Handful of Songs* and *Little White Bull*. He made his T.V. and stage debuts in 1956 and went on to become an all-round entertainer. *(Published by ISV, no.H14).*

A craze for calypso music allowed Harry Belafonte to record songs from his father's native Jamaica. In 1957, he had chart hits with *Banana Boat Song* (No.3) and *Mary's Boy Child*, which topped the charts for the whole of December – and was re-released for Christmas in subsequent years as well. *(Published by Druck, no.174).*

Born Harry Webb in Lucknow in 1940, Cliff Richard returned to England with his family after India's independence. After leaving school, he first joined a skiffle group and then formed a rock 'n' roll trio. He changed his name and signed a recording contract; the first release was *Schoolboy Crush*. However, it was the "B" side, *Move It*, that became his first hit, reaching No.3 in the charts in October 1958. The following year, *Livin' Doll* topped the charts, quickly followed by *Travellin' Light*. In 1958, Cliff had a weekly spot on the ITV show *Oh Boy!* and began by copying Elvis' hip gyrations, described as *"the crudest exhibition ever seen on British TV"!* *(Published by Valex Products, no.VP163).*

Frankie Vaughan's first chart entry was *Green Door* which reached No.2 in November 1956. His next record – *Garden of Eden* – topped the charts for 3 weeks in February 1957, being the most popular of FOUR versions of the song in the charts that month! He had several other hit records in the fifties including *Gotta Have Something in the Bank, Frank*, with the Kaye Sisters. *(Published by Kruger, no.902/79).*

Russ Conway became popular from his appearances on *The Billy Cotton Bandshow.* Despite having had just one piano lesson, he composed (under his own name, T.H. Stanford) and played piano pops to the delight of all ages. His first chart success was *More Party Pops* in 1958. The following year *Sidesaddle* was No.1 for 3 weeks and stayed in the charts for 17 weeks. His other fifties' hits were *Roulette, China Tea* and *Snowcoach*. *(Published by Gary Cards, no.607).*

The last four British charts of the 1950s were topped by the newcomer Adam Faith with *What Do You Want?* He had also started out with a skiffle group and had made his TV debut on *Six-Five Special*. (Published by Kruger, no.902/107).

Pat Boone's first entry in the British charts was with *Ain't that Shame* in November 1955. However, it was his next record be *Home* which was his greatest success and which was regular choice on request programmes for many years come. It was No.1 for six weeks in the summer of 1956. T following year was his best, with five more hits including *L Letters in the Sand* and *April Love*. (Published by Valent real photograph no.39/4)

Home Entertainment
T.V. and Radio

In 1950, most homes had a "wireless" and radio shows drew huge audiences with the most popular programmes attracting more than 20 million listeners. Television, however, was still in its infancy and only available in the London and Midlands areas where just over 300,000 homes had a "box in the corner". Transmitters were erected in other parts of the country so that, by 1953, 50% of the population were within reach of television. The news that the Coronation was to be televised persuaded many people to buy sets for the occasion. The broadcast was so successful that sales of television sets increased by 50% over the next year. A 12-inch screen was a popular size, costing about £70. In 1953, plans for a commercial station were announced, with advertisements restricted to a maximum of 6 minutes per hour. With sales of TV sets escalating, a wider range of programmes was needed. The first British TV "soap opera" was The Grove Family, named after the BBC's Lime Grove Studios and broadcast from April 1954. ITV finally opened to London viewers on 22nd September 1955, for which a new TV set was needed – the older sets could only receive BBC programmes. On that night, the BBC responded by starting earlier and, on the radio, there was a dramatic episode of The Archers with the death of "Grace" in a fire. With so many homes receiving TV, there were the inevitable licence dodgers so, in 1957, the Post Office introduced TV detector vans to retrieve some of their lost revenue. By the end of the decade, the number of people with TV sets had increased to 24$\frac{1}{2}$ million – about two thirds of the population, and we watched for an average of 12$\frac{1}{2}$ hours a week.

A.B.C. TELEVISION STUDIO, DIDSBURY

Independent television spread to the Midlands and North in 1956, having previously only been broadcast in London. The postcard shows the A.B.C. studio in Manchester which provided weekend programmes for the North and Midlands. (weekday programmes were provided by Granada and Associated Television Ltd). The building had been a cinema; on the right, there is a row of outside broadcast vehicles and the posters at the entrance advertise a play in the *Armchair Theatre* series. (Published by Lilywhite Ltd., real photograph no. DBY2).

One of the best-known television advertising campaigns was the Brooke Bond series showing the antics of these chimps, promoting P.G. Tips tea. Their first commercial was broadcast in 1956. Over the years, many famous personalities provided the voices. The chimpanzees were Gene Detroy's Marquis and family and they are seen here at their famous Tea Party. *(Published by Mason's Alpha real photograph no.3).*

"HAVE A GO"   WILFRED PICKLES   BBC COPYRIGHT PHOTOGRAPH

Have a Go was one of the most popular radio shows ever broadcast, with 20 million listeners at its peak. Wilfred Pickles (1904-78) was the host with his wife, Mabel, "at the table", looking after the prize money. Broadcast from 1947 until 1967, it was a live show visiting locations all over Britain. All interviewees took part in a short quiz for which there was a small cash prize – 10/-. Wilfred Pickles was voted the Radio Personality of 1952. In 1954, the couple also hosted a TV programme *Ask Pickles* which was a mixture of unusual talents, the fulfillment of people's dreams and the re-uniting of long lost friends and relatives. *(Published by Photowork Ltd.)*

HESSARY TOR TV MAST, PRINCETOWN

By 1959, TV transmitters had been built to serve most areas of the UK. Although this view is of Princetown, they were obviously so thrilled to receive TV that the mast gets top billing on this postcard! The mast transmitted BBC programmes – ITV was still only broadcast to 7½ million homes. The popularity of television did not please everyone. In 1954, the Pope had warned that television was a potential threat to family life. It was also blamed for the decline in attendance which resulted in the closure of 800 cinemas during the fifties. Illustrated magazines, such as *Picture Post,* closed down, as did commercial lending libraries. Radio lost many listeners and had to revamp the schedules. Television's mix of news, variety, drama films, documentaries and children's programmes was what most people wanted – it was here to stay. *(Published by Photomation Ltd., real photograph no.PLC128).*

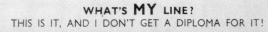

Based on an American show, the BBC bought the rights to *What's My Line?* for 25 guineas. The first programme was in July 1951, with a panel of Marghanita Laski, Jerry Desmonde, Elizabeth Allen and Gilbert Harding. Challengers who beat the panel received a diploma – a far cry from the prizes awarded today. It was voted "the outstanding TV programme": in 1952. Hosted by Eamonn Andrews, there was soon a regular panel of David Nixon, Isobel Barnett, Barbara Kelly and Gilbert Harding. The programme ran until 1963. The title became a national catchphrase and this is just one of several comic cards to use it. *(Posted in Chapel-en-le-Frith, July, 1954; published by Bamforth & Co. Ltd., no.1094).*

Another programme hosted by Eamonn Andrews was *This is Your Life*, first shown by the BBC in July 1955. The first planned programme had to be shelved when the secret script was leaked and the *Daily Sketch* revealed that the subject of the programme was to be footballer Stanley Matthews. A substitute "victim" was quickly chosen, whom Eamonn believed would be boxer Freddie Mills. Eamonn was astonished when the tables were turned and he found himself to be the subject of the big red book! (Posted in Bridlington, July 1959; published by Bamforth & Co. Ltd., no. 1602).

"Bubbles" is the title of this card of a little girl engrossed by a simple pastime. In those days, the bubble liquid was packaged in a small screw-top tin, with a metal ring to blow and catch the bubbles. *(Published by Jarrold & Sons Ltd.).*

WE LOVES TO VIEW — DO YOU?

Arnold Taylor worked for Bamforth, the Holmfirth postcard publishers, for many years. In the 1950s and '60s, he designed a series of postcards for children entitled "Taylor Tots". The designs show children enjoying various activities and included many innovations from those years - from TV to pop music and flower power. The TV programme on this card is unmistakable - *Muffin the Mule*. One of the first children's programmes to be broadcast, in 1946, he was always a favourite character. The puppet was operated by Ann Hogarth, while Annette Mills played the piano on which the puppets performed. The programme continued to amuse children until its final broadcast in 1955. *(Posted in Tarporley, March 1953; published by Bamforth & Co. Ltd., no. K137).*

A day out was a real treat! Wicksteed Park is just outside Kettering and has amenities to please all ages. The children in this picture are all thoroughly enjoying their ride on the "Children's Motor Cars" which followed a track through a beautifully-kept garden. Other attractions in the Park included a miniature railway, paddling pool, model boat lake and ponies. *(Published by Photochrom Co. Ltd., no. C5532).*

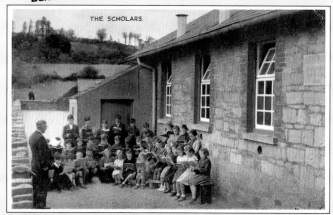

The National School in rural Ireland is typical of many village primary schools in the fifties. Built in the nineteenth century, they usually had lofty, draughty classrooms with wooden floors that could be divided by screens when necessary. Many still had outside toilets - often at the farthest corner of the playground! Infants and juniors would be taught separately, as the juniors had to work for the dreaded eleven-plus examination. *(Posted in Dublin, September 1959; published by E.T.W. Dennis & Sons Ltd.).*

In 1957, there were 448,000 guides in Britain, and membership increased by 100,000 by the end of the decade. Lady Baden-Powell, the founder, was still the Chief Guide. This postcard was printed for the Girl Guides Association in 1954. It shows British guides donating pennies to help purchase equipment and training for guides in refugee camps and countries overtaken by disaster.

"HAVE JUST ARRIVED!"

"I WISH I COULD STAY ON HERE!"

Dan Dare, *"Pilot of the Future,"* arrived at the beginning of the decade. The story appeared on the front of the first edition of the *Eagle* comic on 14th April 1950. The 2-page serial was created and drawn by Frank Hampson (1918-85), who built models of spaceships and cities to make his drawings accurate from any angle. He also researched current space technology on which to base his stories. The *Eagle* was the brainchild of Hampson and Rev. Marcus Morris, who disapproved of the American comics that were imported after the war. It was published by Hulton Press and was their first comic. *(Published by Valentine, no. 5098).*

Another series from the *Eagle*, *Riders of the Range*, featured the adventures of cowboy Jeff Arnold - seated on the fence - and his sidekick, Luke - unseated on the left! An interesting detail is the cigarette in the hero's right hand. The early comic strips were in colour, drawn by Harry Bishop, whilst the later, black and white ones were drawn by various artists. *(Published by Valentine no. 5094).*

Skiffle your blues away!

THOMAS THE TANK ENGINE has brought some passengers for Bertie the 'Bus

Children will always try to copy the latest trend and, with skiffle, this was quite easy. New washing machines meant many discarded washboards to produce the true skiffle sound. Teenagers formed groups with just a washboard, a tea chest with broom handle and string, and one member rich enough to possess a guitar. This picture was drawn by Dinah, who specialised in designs of children. *(Posted in Brentwood, July 1958; published by Mason's Alpha, Dinah Series no. 12/3).*

MISTY, the grey pony, pays a visit to the Blacksmith

The well-known railway books written by Rev. W. Awdry were published from 1946 onwards. The books were very popular with children and adults alike and their success prompted the publisher, Edmund Ward Ltd., to issue some of the illustrations as postcards in the 1950s. This card is from *Thomas the Tank Engine*, illustrated by C. Reginald Dalby who produced the drawings for the first eleven Rev. Awdry books. *(Published by Edmund Ward Ltd., no. 101/1).*

A scene from *The Grey Pony*, published in 1954, one of a series of informative books for children, issued in Ward's *Truth in a Tale* series. The pony book was written and illustrated by John T. Kenney (1911-72), who also provided the illustrations for books 12-17 of the Rev. Awdry series. *(Published by Edmund Ward Ltd. no. 501/19).*

Harry Corbett was a businessman with a degree in engineering. On holiday in Blackpool in 1948 he came across a glove puppet and bought it to entertain his children – little did he know what it would lead to! They first appeared on TV in 1952 for a fee of £10 per programme. The card shows the props that were used – the toy xylophone and stick, a hammer and the magic wand which was used with the words *"Izzy Wizzy, let's get busy"*. Poor Harry always got the worst of things and was often squirted with water or covered with flour and usually received a blow to the head from one of the props! So popular was this naughty little bear that Harry's fingers were said to be insured for £20,000. In 1957, an even naughtier puppet, Sweep, joined the act. The programmes usually ended in total chaos with an exasperated-sounding Harry saying *"Bye-bye children"*. The postcard has a facsimile signature stamped on it and was probably a promotional item.

George Cansdale is seen here feeding the penguins at Sandown Zoo, which opened in July 1955. He was well-known for his popular children's television programme *Looking at Animals* which had been broadcast since 1953. It was an informative programme, shown at teatime, just before the so-called "toddler's truce" – the interlude between 6-7 p.m., when TV closed down to enable children to be put to bed! Interludes also appeared in the TV schedules at other times. These were usually about 5 minutes in duration and short films were shown to fill the gap – the potter's wheel, speeded-up railway journey, kitten and wool and a windmill were the most popular of the fourteen films used. *(Published by W.J. Nigh, real photograph no.5509).*

Westerns seemed to capture the entertainment world in the Fifties. There were hundreds of western films made for the cinema, several series for television, and books and comics for all ages. In 1958, *Wagon Train* was first shown on British TV. This starred Ward Bond as the boss and Robert Horton as the scout - seen here. It quickly became a top-ratings series and was so popular that, when the 1959 General Election was held on the sme day as the programme, the Labour Party feared that their supporters might not turn out to vote for fear of missing their favourite show! (Published by Gary Cards, no. 604).

"I wish you wouldn't twiddle the knob, George, just when things are getting exciting!"

The famous postcard artist Donald McGill was frequently taken to court by seaside watch committees for his risqué humour. This is a typical example of his postcard wit, with a television used to provide a *double entendre*. Hubert sent it from Porthcawl in August 1954 to Mrs Phipps at Cinderford *"to cheer you."*('New McGill' comic, published by D. Constance).

The White Heather Club was first shown on BBC television in 1958. It featured Scottish music and performers and introduced Andy Stewart to the rest of Britain. Other regulars were Robin Hall and Jimmie MacGregor, and Jim MacLeod's Scottish Dance Band. The postcard shows the Band, attired in tartan jackets, with Jim MacLeod at the piano, on the stage of the Dunblane Hydro where they were the resident dance band. *(Published by The White Heather Publishing Co. Ltd., no.481).*

Sport and Recreation

At the beginning of the decade, recreational facilities were rather limited. For many people, sport was simply part of the school curriculum and, after leaving school or college, was only continued if a person had a particular interest or flair for it. Public facilities were few and far between and some sports still had a "middle-class" image such as golf, sailing, skiing and lawn tennis. The increase in the number of university and college students who were offered the chance to participate in a wide range of sports and outdoor activities, plus television coverage of many sports, encouraged people to seek out or demand better facilities. By the end of the decade, a few enlightened local councils had built – or had plans for – sports centres to provide "sport for all".

One outdoor activity that was well-catered for was bowls. Most towns had at least one bowling green and probably several teams competing in local leagues. Being a game of skill, it has always been enjoyed by people of all ages. In Britain, it can be traced back to the thirteenth century – long before Sir Francis Drake insisted on finishing his game at Plymouth. There are 2 or 3 games in progress on this green at Hornsea's Victoria Gardens. As usual, the green is surrounded by beautiful gardens where a player's friends and family can sit and watch. The building behind is the Marine Hotel. *(Posted in Hornsea, August 1955; published by ARJAY Productions, real photograph no. 162.82).*

The outdoor swimming pool or lido was a very popular venue – and not just in summer. Not only resorts, but also many towns and cities, had an open-air baths complex. Keepers' Pool is just one of the many stretches of water in Sutton Park, Sutton Coldfield. The other pools were set aside for sailing, rowing and paddling, and boats and canoes could be hired. The changing rooms for swimmers line the poolside on the left. There are a lot of people about and most of the spectators are wearing sun hats so it must have been a hot day. The picture probably dates from the early fifties but was not posted until 1962. *(Published by Valentine, real photograph no.H1499).*

"Outward bound" was the name given to this sea school at Aberdovey, founded by Kurt Hahn, in 1941. The Outward Bound Trust was formed in 1946 to establish residential schools for boys and girls, where they would learn mountaineering as well as naval and other outdoor activities. This postcard shows youngsters at the original school; in the bottom pictures they are launching and rowing a boat and in the top pictures, canoeing and map-reading – with the help of a dog! The sender of this card does not mention the course, just the cold and snow which had lasted all week. A message on a card from another Outward Bound School indicates just how rigorous the training was – *"Just finished P.T. ... had to CRAWL up the stairs to my dormitory"!* (Posted in Aberdovey, 1959; published by Pickfords, real photograph no.2).

For anyone contemplating taking up gliding, this promotional card could have been the final encouragement. Most of the views were taken from the air and show the local scenery. The central bottom view shows the club's hangar, and members busy with repair work. Gliding as a sport began before World War 1, with the first British club being the Amberley Aviation Society, founded in 1912. In the 1950s, several World War 2 airfields were abandoned and being ideal locations for gliding clubs, the sport really "took off"! *(no publisher indicated).*

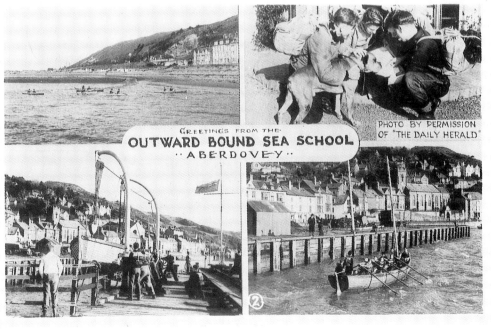

MISS PAT SMYTHE ON "MR. POLLARD" 26453

THE FIRING POINT. (ASHBURTON DAY) CENTURY RANGE. BISLEY

Pat Smythe was a top British rider throughout the 1950s. She represented Great Britain at the Olympic Games in 1956, being a member of the Show Jumping Team. Although the 1956 summer Olympics were held in Melbourne, the equestrian events took place in Stockholm because of the very strict Australian quarantine rules. British teams won gold medals for the 3-day event and dressage competitions, and a bronze in the show jumping. Pat Smythe was the first woman to win an equestrian medal. She also won several competitions on this horse – *Mr. Pollard* – and throughout her show jumping career won titles all over the world. At the same time, she wrote many books – both fact and fiction – with an equestrian theme. *(Real photograph no.26453, no publisher indicated).*

Bisley, Surrey, is the home of the National Rifle Association and boasts some very fine rifle ranges. The postcard shows competitors on Ashburton Day – there are so many taking part that the line stretches almost out of sight! Seated behind are the marshals, scrutineers and scorekeepers. The blackboards chart the teams' progress – the ones nearest the camera are for Rugby, Aldenham and Canford schools. The card was sent by a competitor who *"...did no good this year...".* (Posted in Bisley, July 1958; published by Gale & Polden Ltd., real photograph no.146).

One of the Royal Family's favourite events – the Highland Games at Braemar – is shown on this card. Tossing the caber – a tapering tree trunk – not only requires great strength but also good judgement as it has to strike the ground in such a way as to fall directly opposite the competitor. (*posted in Braemar, August 1958; published by J. Arthur Dixon, no.3673*).

Denis Compton was vice-captain of Middlesex in 1950-51. He made his Test debut in 1937 and played in a further 77 Test matches – scoring 5,807 runs – before he retired in 1957. A great batsman, he made 123 centuries in his first-class career. In 1953, he scored the winning run to regain the Ashes in the fifth Test at the Oval. Cricket was not his only sport; he also played soccer for Arsenal, gaining a league medal in 1947-8, an F.A. Cup winners medal in 1950, and represented England in 1943. *(Published by Valentine, real photograph no. R.P.52).*

DENIS C. S. COMPTON (MIDDLESEX)

G. MERRICK.

Birmingham born and bred, Gilbert Merrick joined Birmingham City from Solihull Town in 1939. He was 6ft tall, weighed 13 stone and was a brilliant goalkeeper in the post-war years. He took over the England goal in 1951, and appeared for England 23 times. For his club, he was instrumental in helping the team gain promotion and, from 1946 until he retired in 1959, he appeared for Birmingham City on 486 occasions. According to the information on the back of this postcard he was *"...distinguished as one of the few footballers wearing a moustache..."* (Published by Valentine, real photograph no. R.P.67).

"ALFA ROMEO."

Alfa Romeo—Formula 1.—Manufactured in Italy. 2 stage supercharged engine. Speed in region of 150-160 m.p.h. Winner of many Continental Grand Prix racing events. Drivers: Fangio and Farina.

Italian Guiseppe Farina (1909-66) won the inaugural World Drivers Championship in 1950, driving an Alfa Romeo. To gain the title he had won the British, Italian and Swiss Grand Prix races. Also driving for Alfa Romeo was the runner-up in that first championship – the brilliant Argentinian, Juan Fangio, who went on to win the title in 1951 – again driving for Alfa Romeo. In the early fifties Italian cars reigned supreme in Grand Prix racing and in 1950 the Alfa Romeo Type 158, the "Alfetta", was the fastest car around with an average speed of 150-160 m.p.h. In 1950, Alfa Romeo had won all the races on the Grand Prix circuit, but by 1952 they were facing a strong challenge from Ferrari and announced their withdrawal from Grand Prix racing. *(Posted in West Hartlepool, November 1954; published by Valentine, no.5002).*

"H.W.M."

H.W.M.—Formula 11—1960 c.c. Alta engine. Manufactured in Great Britain. Speed in region of 130-140 m.p.h. The 1951 H.W.M. competed in 15 Continental races finishing all well to the fore. Drivers: Stirling Moss, Lance Macklin, Duncan Hamilton.

A young Stirling Moss had dominated the 500cc class in the late 1940s, so went on to Formula 2 cars in the early 1950s. He drove this British H.W. Motors car which had a top speed of 130-140 m.p.h. After a successful period he joined Mercedes-Benz in 1955 and won several Grand Prix races, being the first Briton to win the British Grand Prix in 1955, and the only Englishman to win the Mille Miglia – also in 1955. The H.W.M. was raced in the 1952 and 1953 Formula 1 seasons, with drivers Lance Macklin, Duncan Hamilton and Peter Collins. *(Posted in Rochdale, March 1956; published by Valentine no.5004).*

HULL R.F.C. RUGBY LEAGUE CHAMPIONS - 1957-58

A. Holdstock (inset), P. Whiteley, S. Cowan, M. Scott, B. Saville, G. Sharpley (Trainer), G. Dannatt (inset) B. Cooper, C. Cole, C. Sykes, B. Hambling, R. Francis (Coach), J. Whiteley (Capt.), T. Harris, J. Drake, W. Drake C. Turner, P. Bateson, I. Watts, F. Broadhurst, T. Finn, G. Harrison

1956 OLYMPIAD MELBOURNE ○ AUSTRALIA

The Duke of Edinburgh opened the 16th Olympic Games on 22nd November 1956, in Melbourne, Australia; the first time that the Games were held in the southern hemisphere. It was a difficult time for some teams as Anglo-French forces had recently invaded Suez and the Soviet Union crushed the Hungarian uprising just days before the Games started. Some teams felt compelled to withdraw. Britain gained several gold medals:- Chris Brasher's gold medal in the steeplechase was the first British track medal for 26 years; Judy Grinham won the 100m backstroke; Terry Spinks won the flyweight and R. McTaggart the heavyweight boxing and Gillian Sheen took gold in the women's fencing.*(Design by J. Rajko).*

The famous Irish Hospitals' Sweepstake was first organised in 1930. The pictures on this promotional multiview show, clockwise from top left:- *Arctic Prince,* winner of the 1951 Epsom Derby and owned by the Irish Sweeps Chief, Mr. J. McGrath; the Parade at the Dublin Horse Show; ticket counterfoil mixing – in which 160 operatives are engaged; Meet of Hounds at Castletown House and in the centre, a 1958 view of the famous "drum" – no computers here, everything had to be done by hand.

The fifties were a very successful decade for Hull Rugby League Club. They won the championship twice and were runners-up on another occasion, reaching the Challenge Cup Final twice and the Yorkshire Cup Final four times. This 1956-7 Championship-winning side was captained by Johnny Whiteley and included the famous Drake brothers.

Work

After World War 2, there was a boom in British industry as people attempted to replace and renew items that had been unobtainable for years. The demand for goods was only held back by a shortage of labour in the factories and by the limited stocks of raw materials. Once rationing ended in the fifties, there was increased demand for electrical and household goods and for the new ranges of pre-packaged foods.

"BLIMEY! WE CAN DO WITHOUT **AUTOMATION** AT OUR HOUSE, FRED!"

As industrial machinery became outdated or beyond further repair, companies took the opportunity to refit their factories with the latest equipment which was cleaner, quieter, safer and less labour-intensive than in the pre-war years. By the end of the decade, unions had to accept that industry was being revolutionised by automation. The sender of this card does not say whether his job was affected – but he obviously conducted his holiday romances along production line methods: *"...Grass not wet on the cliffs. Changed women three times, had some good fun then left them..."! (Posted at Bridlington in July 1958; Published by Bamforth & Co. Ltd., no.1419).*

Working with food calls for high standards of hygiene so the men here are working on stainless steel tables which are easily cleaned. This is the Meat Preparing Room at Shippam's of Chichester. Around the walls are racks of poultry and the men at the tables are working on joints of ham. These were probably destined for meat pastes or other convenience foods that became so popular in the 1950s. *(Published by Britannia Colour Ltd., no.S.C.1).*

Situated at King's Langley, Hertfordshire, the Ovaltine factory was built in the 1930s. Besides the main building, the card also shows the Dairy and Egg Farms which were built to provide the ingredients for their popular beverage. Most children from the 1950s will remember the Radio Luxembourg programme that the firm sponsored with its opening signature tune – *"We are the Ovaltineys ...". (Posted in Woodford Green, March 1961).*

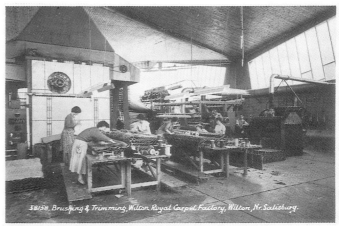

This postcard of the Wilton Royal Carpet Factory shows the contrast between old and new working methods. In the background, two men are overseeing modern looms and machinery – many factories had to upgrade their equipment after the war. In the foreground, the ladies are hard at work brushing and trimming the carpets – tasks that still had to be done by hand. *(Posted in Salisbury; published by Sweetman & Son Ltd., real photograph no.58158).*

Commercial vehicles played an important part in the post-war industrial boom. Firms found it a convenient and profitable way of delivering goods to an ever-increasing population. The vehicles here belong to Shippam's of Chichester and are waiting at the labelling, packing and despatch section of their modern factory. The van on the left is open and is presumably being loaded. The detail on the card is not very clear but the vans seem to be (from left to right) an Atkinson, a Morris and an Austin. The vehicles are small compared to modern juggernauts. In 1955, the largest vehicles were only 35ft in length and the heaviest lorries were still only permitted to travel at a maximum speed of 20 m.p.h. on our roads! The motorway network was soon to change all that! *(Published by Britannia Colour Ltd., no.S.C.6).*

Shopping

The hated ration book was still much in evidence at the beginning of the decade. As supplies increased, rationing was gradually phased out; clothes and tinned food in 1949; soap – July 1950; tea – October 1952; chocolate and sweets – July 1953; sugar – September 1953; coke fuel – February 1954; margarine, butter, fats and cheese – May 1954; meat and bacon – July 1954 and, finally, coal in July 1958. With the freedom to buy any goods they wanted, customers expected a wider range of products to choose from, so shops were forced to increase their shelf space. Supermarkets and self-service helped to cater for the growing army of shoppers and by the end of the decade, many towns had decided to build new "shopping centres" to satisfy the new consumer society.

This fruit stall on London's embankment has a very tempting choice of fresh produce on show. The picture dates from c.1956 and the prices that are visible offer apples at 1/8d (8p) per pound, pears at 1/10d (9p) per pound, cherries at 2/6d (12½p) per pound (he's almost sold out of those!) and roasted peanuts at 6d (2½p) per pound. At the time an average wage was less than £10 per week. (Published by Valentine, no. T.33).

The market square in Llanrwst is thronged with shoppers on this view. It looks like a fine, sunny day but there is hardly a head without a hat! The stall in the foreground has roll upon roll of patterned linoleum - the usual floor covering for the early fifties - for sale. The Town Hall dominates the Square. (Published by Photochrom Co. Ltd, real photograph no. 79312).

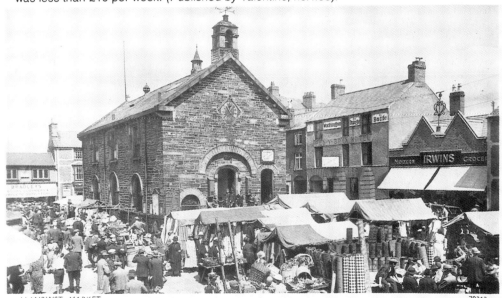

LLANRWST. MARKET.   79312

HIGH STREET, BRIDGNORTH

The clock on Bridgnorth's half-timbered Town Hall reads ten to three, and there are signs that the Saturday market traders are starting to pack up their stalls. The ones nearest the camera have some fruit and vegetables left, while the large covered stall in the centre has clothes on its rails. The High Street is very busy, with no space left to park. Set on arches, the Town Hall straddles the High Street, and a furniture van is just squeezing its way through. (Card posted in Bridgnorth; published by Valentine, no. L9142).

LLANFAIRPWLLGWYNGYLLGOGERYCHWYRNDROBWLL-LLANTYSILIOGOGOGOCH
Church/Mary /a Hollow/White /Hazel/ close to / the / rapid / whirlpool / Church / St. Tysilio / Cave / Red.
40210

A village store is always a vital part of a community. It looks as if this newsagents and confectionery shop had gradually encroached on the rest of the buildings on the ground floor. The main shop window is full of large sweet jars and there are advertisements for *Wizard* and *Astra* fireworks. The other windows have displays of souvenirs – some with the village's famous long name – and toys and books including the *Swift* and other annuals. Outside, the board advertises the *Radio Times* and there are vending machines for *Beech Nut* chewing gum – 1d a pack – and cigarettes. The walls and windows have lots of advertisements, mostly for cigarettes. *(Published by St. Albans series, real photograph no.40210).*

This row of shops in Burgess Hill, Sussex, is typical of those built in many British towns in the fifties. Retail space is on the ground floor with flats above and a lay-by for parking outside. The shops look fairly new here. The largest is a branch of Woolworth's and, next door, is an International Stores with signs in the windows announcing that it is a self service shop. *(Published by Shoesmith & Etheridge Ltd., real photograph no. D13711).*

CHURCH ROAD, BURGESS HILL.   D 13711

Above Bar, Southampton

23344

In cities, larger shopping developments were built. These were often occupied by branches of the well-known chain stores which were to take over every high street. Above Bar was the main shopping street of Southampton and had to be rebuilt after bomb damage in World War 2; the Bargate – seen in the distance – survived. British Home Stores has a window display of typical fifties dresses – slim waists and full skirts over a net petticoat. On the right, a queue of weary shoppers wait for the bus home. *(Published by J. Salmon Ltd., Photostyle no.23344).*

Rebuilding

Many British cities suffered considerable bomb damage during World War 2 and this necessitated a great deal of rebuilding in the early post-war years. Where bombs had caused most destruction, whole areas were cleared and new centres built on the site. The cities worst affected were Bristol, Coventry, Exeter, Hull, Liverpool, Plymouth, Southampton and London.

THE ROYAL PARADE, PLYMOUTH.

PARAGON SQUARE, HULL.

The centre of Plymouth was cleared of its bomb-damaged buildings and became the site of much new development. This is the Royal Parade containing many new shops, with Dingle's store at the far end. This view, taken c.1953, shows sparkling white pavements with newly-planted trees and flower-beds. There are few private vehicles but plenty of buses. Out of sight, to the right of this view, is St. Andrew's Church whose badly damaged shell was retained and later restored; also on the right, the new Civic Centre development was built in the late 1950s and early 1960s. *(Published by Valentine, no.K5070).*

Hull suffered a great deal of bomb damage which necessitated the rebuilding of most of the city centre. The new wide streets included many flower-beds and lawned areas. This view of Paragon Square shows the impressive War Memorial with neat gardens around it. Behind the Memorial, the buildings house the Midland and Barclays Banks. On the left is one of the city's large department stores – Hammonds. Also visible are the old overhead tram wires – but no tracks – as the trams were replaced by trolleybuses in 1945. *(Published by Valentine, no.L943).*

Boring postcards? By the fifties, seaside comics and tourist views were the staples of picture postcard retailing, yet, as this book shows, there was still a wide variety of cards available. While it would be difficult to argue that picture postcards reflected every aspect of life - as they undoubtedly had done in the "Golden Age" - they certainly provide a fascinating snapshot of a decade when life was less hurried and complicated than it is now, yet was developing and changing at ever-increasing speed. A recently-published book focused on 'boring' postcards of the decade - yet the examples here give a vibrant picture of Fifties life.

BROADGATE HOUSE, COVENTRY.

This view of the first stage of the Broadgate development in Coventry was taken from the tower of the Cathedral which was the only part of that building left standing after the air raids of 1940. The layout of the reconstructed part of the city was partly based on an imaginative plan that had been drawn up before the outbreak of war. The new design was prepared by the city architect, Donald Gibson, and the city engineer. On the right of the picture, behind the bus, is the site of the next phase of Broadgate – still a rubble-strewn area here. *(Posted in Coventry, May 1959; real photograph no.28).*

This is St. Oswald's Church on Coventry's Tile Hill estate. It was designed by Basil Spence who had won the open competition to design a new cathedral for the city. He also designed similar churches for the other two housing estates of the New Coventry plan – Willenhall and Bell Green. All three buildings were paid for from the war-damage grant for one of the central city churches that was destroyed. Some of the new houses on the estate can just be seen on the right. *(Published by Gordon Fraser, real photograph no. AT02-10).*

Town and Country

In St. Albans, the Town Hall faces the wide thoroughfare of St. Peter's Street, which is also the site of the market on Saturdays. On this early 1950s view, a sign on the Town Hall facade announces the sale of tickets for St. Albans Pageant. There are lots of people shopping and on the right a Post Office Telephone van is just one of many contemporary vehicles parked on the street. With easy access to London by road and rail, St. Albans had grown from a city of just 7,000 inhabitants in 1851 to a population of 46,000 in 1957. *(Published in the St. Alban's series, real photograph no.2377).*

The tall tower of Derby cathedral, at 178ft, was higher than any other building in the town in the 1950s. (Derby was not designated as a city until 1977, but All Saints Parish Church was raised to cathedral status in 1927). This bustling scene in the Market Square shows a mixture of pre and post-war vehicles – cars, vans, lorries, buses and a trolleybus with an advertisement for *Corona*. The large store on the corner of Irongate is that of Barlow, Taylor & Co. Ltd.; their window displays of dress fabrics and millinery are hidden by the awnings which are fully extended against the bright sunlight. On the left is a branch of Cantor's furniture store; next door is Austin Hodgkinson's shop and Foulds' and W. Hackney's shops can be seen. *(Posted in Derby, August 1952; published by Photochrom Co. Ltd., real photograph no. 85433).*

Right in the centre of Manchester, Piccadilly Gardens offers a welcome respite to weary shoppers and travellers. This early 1950s view was taken on a lovely sunny day but there are few people about. The bus station is fairly busy with vehicles ready to carry passengers to all corners of the city – and beyond. On the left, the tracks and overhead wires of the old tram system are still visible. The large shop beyond the bus station is Lewis's department store. *(Published by Raphael Tuck, real photograph no.MH32).*

The bus has a clear road ahead as it makes its way south down English Street, Carlisle. Behind it, the statue of James Steel and old Carlisle Cross mark the traditional centre of the city, in front of the unassuming Town Hall. Here, the area is a main bus stop, with smart new shelters and queues of people waiting for buses. The low level of traffic allows pedestrians to cross the road freely – as, indeed, they can today, as the whole area has been pedestrianised. *(Posted in Carlisle, June 1959; published by E.T.W. Dennis, Photoblue no. C0706.L).*

PIER HEAD AND RIVER MERSEY, LIVERPOOL.

After World War Two the British towns and cities that still had a tramcar service were faced with the cost of replacing or repairing track and trams that were in poor condition. Because the system lacked flexibility, many places decided that their trams should gradually be phased out. In our largest cities, systems lasted for a few more years and were still a familiar sight – and sound – on the streets. The last London trams ran in 1952, Birmingham's in 1953 and Liverpool's in 1957, whilst in Sheffield and Glasgow the trams survived until 1960 and 1962 respectively. The postcard shows Liverpool trams in c.1950, waiting at the well-known Pierhead, where a ferry boat is just about to dock. *(Published by Valentine, phototype no.H7645).*

At Chingford Mount, two trolleybuses on route 699 wait to begin their next journey, whilst their drivers stand chatting on the pavement. In the foreground, a queue of people waits for a trolleybus going in the opposite direction. The poles carrying the wires to supply electric power to the trolley arms dominate the street scene. In many areas, trolleybuses had replaced trams as they were more manoeuvrable, quieter and did not require tracks. However, they were frequently found to be an obstruction on busy routes and were gradually replaced by motor buses. In London, the changeover began in 1953 – but the last trolleybus was not withdrawn until 1962. *(Posted in London, April 1955; published by Raphael Tuck, real photograph no.CF3).*

CF 3   ALBERT CRESCENT, CHINGFORD MOUNT   A TUCK CARD

EG 4   EGREMONT BUS STATION AT SEACOMBE FERRY

This is the Wallasey Corporation bus station at Seacombe Ferry, with part of its fleet of Leyland buses. When the boat arrived from Liverpool, hundreds of people would board these buses to local destinations on the Wirral peninsula. In urban areas, the bus was the most efficient way to transport large numbers of passengers. Every corporation had its own fleet of buses and most of these would be British-built. *(Published by Tokim Productions, real photograph no.E.G.4).*

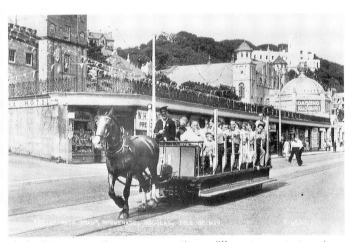

In holiday areas, there are sometimes different ways to travel – cliff lifts, pier and miniature railways and various types of tram. This postcard shows the unique horse-tram service, begun in August 1876, which carries passengers along Douglas promenade. They are called "toast rack" trams because the bench seats are arranged like the partitions on a breakfast table toast rack. This tram, no.31, is full of relaxed holidaymakers enjoying the views over Douglas Bay. They are just passing the Castle Mona Hotel, on the left. In the distance, a poster announces a show starring the "Dancing Squadronnaires". *(Published by Valentine, real photograph no.R4830).*

Transport – Traffic

At the beginning of the 1950s, traffic was not a serious problem on the streets of our towns and cities. Except for peak times, traffic moved at a reasonable rate and it was usually possible to park on the street. There is very little traffic on this view of Boscawen Street, Truro. The cars on the right are parked outside the "Red Lion Hotel". The pavements are glistening after a recent rain shower – which probably explains why there are so few pedestrians. (Published by Dearden and Wade, real photograph, no.1932).

By the mid-fifties it seemed that – in our cities at least – everyone wanted to be in the same place at the same time! The increase in the number of private motorists meant that it was more difficult to park on the street and, when driving, progress was slow as pedestrians and parked vehicles were a constant hazard. This view of High Street, Canterbury, shows the congestion that was common in a modern shopping area. Despite the signs pointing to a car park, there are parked vehicles on both sides of the street and if there was a pedestrian crossing, it seems that these pedestrians had no intention of using it! (Published by Shoesmith & Etheridge Ltd., real photograph no. D/12047).

HIGH STREET FROM ST. GEORGE'S GATE, CANTERBURY. D/12047

EASTGATE CHESTER W 8075

By 1959, city traffic was posing real problems. In the older cities, with narrow streets – as in this view of Eastgate Street, Chester – traffic jams were a common occurrence. Parked vehicles and buses picking up and putting down their passengers impeded the flow of through traffic. In the middle of this picture, a policeman tries in vain to keep the traffic moving. In some cases, a ring road would be built to remove through traffic from the central shopping areas, whilst extra car parks were provided for shoppers and visitors. (Posted in Chester, May 1959; published by Valentine, real photograph no. W8075).

The reason for this traffic-free stretch of Moston Lane, near Manchester, can be understood by closer inspection of this picture. Both sides of the road have been painted with yellow lines – a continuous one on the left and a broken line on the right. A sign on the lamppost indicates restriction times. The first yellow lines were painted in Slough and were effective from February, 1956; they were gradually introduced to towns and cities throughout the country. (Published by Lilywhite Ltd., real photograph no. MSN3).

Moston Lane, Moston   MSN 3

Looking towards Ashbourne's famous "Cathedral of the Peak", this view shows a busy scene in St. John Street – with a Jowett car driving away from the camera. In the left foreground is the *"Green Man & Black's Head Hotel"*, with its entrance to a courtyard beyond. When this card was posted, bed and breakfast at the Hotel cost 22/6, with dinner being an additional 10/6d. The town's population had increased from 3,810 in 1851 to 5,480 in the 1950s. The town is famous for its gingerbread and also for the annual Shrove Tuesday football match – where the goals are 3 miles apart, rules are few and any number can take part. *(Posted in Ashbourne, August 1959; published by Valentine, real photograph no. K9765).*

Despite the proximity of London, Epping is still a small market town with the population being just 8,500 in the late 1950s. This is part of the long High Street at the Market Place. St. John's Church is just out of sight on the left. The building on the left of the picture is Barclay's Bank and, a little nearer the camera, a builder's lorry is parked beside some scaffolding where building work is in progress. In front of the shops on the right, the parked cars include a Sunbeam, Vauxhall, Wolseley and Morris – all lined up as if on show. *(Posted in London, June 1955; published by Fitzwilliams, real photograph no.2117).*

Fermoy is a small market town in the Irish Republic. In the middle of the nineteenth century, the population was over 8,000, but by the 1950s it had dropped to less than 4,000 inhabitants. The shops on the left include Abernethy's confectionery, McCabe's shoe shop and O'Keefe's store. The photograph is so clear that it is possible to read most of the vehicle registration numbers. The card was sent in 1957, by a holidaymaker who was entranced with this corner of Ireland. *(Published by Cardall Ltd., real photograph).*

Market days in Newton Abbot were on Wednesdays and Saturdays – this picture was probably taken on one of these days as there are a couple of stalls on the right-hand side of the street. There are plenty of shoppers here, making their way down Market Street, heading for Market Square. On the right is J. Gibson's grocery with the Trustee Savings Bank beyond. Outside the Bank, there is a lorry which seems to be decorated like a carnival float. *(Published by Graham C. Newstead, real photograph).*

There is an interesting assortment of vehicles on this view of High Street, Shoreham, taken at 9.45 a.m. – if the clock over Davey's shop is correct! This is in the modern town which is separated from old Shoreham by the River Adur and Shoreham Beach. On the right is the old flint and stone building housing the Marlipins Museum and, next door, the Marlipins public house. Beyond that, the Pickwick Restaurant has a "For Sale" notice on it. Shoreham had grown considerably since the census of 1851 – from a population of 2,590 to 14,650. The card was sent by a holidaymaker who expected to have *"...great difficulty in tearing ourselves away – in fact we are considering retiring early!".* (Posted in Lancing, August 1959; real photograph no. 26166).

This view of Bridge Street, Sunderland, features a queue of traffic that contains a wide variety of vehicles from the early fifties. A private car is followed by a delivery van belonging to Christie Malcolm Ltd, printers; a double decker bus; a tram with an advertisement for Binns and a single decker bus. In the distance is Wearmouth Bridge, built in 1929. The tall building on the right is the *"Grand Hotel"*, a 3-star establishment where bed and breakfast would have cost 45/-, with dinner an extra 10/6d. Opposite is the *"Central Hotel"* and Walkers, Jewellers' shop on the corner of High Street West. The nineteenth century was a time of growth and increased trade so that the population swelled, from 67,394 in 1851, to 182,900 a century later. *(Published by Valentine, real photograph no.H138).*

Fore Street, Trowbridge, is believed to follow the curves of the old ditch and rampart that surrounded the castle that once stood here. When this photograph was taken it was a quiet, one-way street. The vehicles on the left are parked outside the *"George Hotel"* a 2-star establishment with 20 bedrooms. Next door is the Midland Bank and premises of the Sun Insurance Office Ltd. On the right is the shop of Lewis Darling, with a window full of smart shirts and an advertisement for Jaeger products; the adjacent shop is an electrical store. *(Posted in Bath, August 1959; published by Sweetman & Son Ltd., real photograph no. 54236).*

Wem, a small market town in Shropshire, suffered a great fire in 1667, which destroyed most of the town. However, the 14th century tower on the parish church survived and can just be seen in the distance, on this view of the High Street. On the left is a chemist's shop with scaffolding at the front; further up the street, the "White Horse" public house is selling *Wem Ales*, a well-known local brew; adjacent to it is a branch of Bradleys, the local chain of clothiers. On the right, Gordon Rhodes' shop has goods displayed outside, and advertisements for several brands of cigarettes:- *Players, Capstan, Gold Flake, Bristol.* Judging by the goods on display, he sold everything from footballs to clothes - and probably this postcard, as his name appears on the front as the publisher.

Villages

Joys Green, Lydbrook is on the edge of the Forest of Dean. The photograph was taken whilst new houses were being built on the hill opposite – which is now covered in houses. On the right, the white, single-storey buildings are "prefabs", which were so welcome to the many families affected by the chronic post-war housing shortage. In some areas, these "temporary" homes have survived but those on this card were replaced by bungalows. A local bus company garaged its fleet of coaches and double decker buses in an old aeroplane hangar, which is just out of sight on the left; the little building in the open space is a bus shelter. (Published by Lilywhite, real photograph no.LBK.6).

All the shops on the right-hand side of this picture of High Street, Cemaes Bay, Anglesey, have been converted from private dwellings and if it were not for the advertising signs, it would be difficult to tell they were shops. In the right foreground, the general store has all manner of goods on display and a sign above for *"Raleigh – The all style bicycle"*. The children outside are watching the photographer with interest! The white cottages are three different shops; the first is R. Michael's with a "Hovis" sign attached to the wall; next is a confectioners' and newsagent but the only identifiable part of the third shop is the awning over the window. Beyond the white cottages are two further shops. There is an inn at the end of the street and another shop on the left, which has a rack of postcards outside. *(Posted in Cemaes Bay, July 1956; published by Frith & Co., real photograph, no.CB135).*

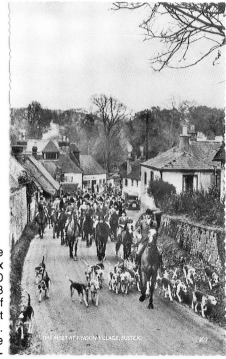

Totley Rise is five miles south of Sheffield, close to the Derbyshire border. This very clear photograph was taken on a lovely sunny day, when many people were out shopping. The shops that can be identified are, from the right, Gratton's, a wines, spirits and provisions merchant selling Stones Cannon Ales; E. Jackson, Post Office; J. Shentall Ltd., which seems to have a queue stretching right out onto the pavement; R. Damm's fruit and vegetable shop; a cafe; and Parkinson's hardware shop. Several contemporary vehicles complete the picture. The card was not sent until 1963, when the writer described Totley as a *"very pleasant district"*. *(Published by A.W. Bourne, real photograph).*

The small village of Findon, Sussex – a mere 900 inhabitants in 1958 – lies just west of the Iron Age hill-fort of Cissbury Ring. Fortunately, the main road by-passes the narrow village streets. So many people have turned out for this meet of the local hunt that the narrow street is filled with their horses as far as the eye can see. It was obviously a calm winter's day, as the plumes of smoke from the cottage chimneys drift straight up into the sky. The card was not posted until 1963, when the writer explained that this was her sister's "shopping centre"! *(Published by A.W. Wardell, real photograph no.203).*

JOHN O'GROATS HOUSE HOTEL 5   *Copyright—J. Adams*

Tourist spots

Places that attract large numbers of tourists have to make extra provision for their visitors. Not only will tourists require accommodation and food, but also parking places for coaches and cars – and there were so many more cars in the 1950s. To cater for this increase in demand, tourist towns allocated extra land for parking and many local people opened bed and breakfast establishments, restaurants and souvenir shops – selling local postcards, of course!

To stay in this hotel in 1958, the charge was 17/6d for bed and breakfast. There were 20 bedrooms but just 3 baths. This popular spot was obviously short of parking space when this photograph was taken as cars, coaches and vans are parked all over the grass. In 1957, the travel writer G. Douglas Bolton complained that *"tourists pour out in droves ... produce sheaves of picture postcards, feverishly write as many as possible to show that they have been there and then retire exhausted to the waiting coaches, having seen nothing of John O'Groats".* (Published by J. Adams, real photograph no.5, and posted at John O'Groats in July 1963).

On a summer's day in Keswick, the Main Street car park is full, Holidaymakers crowd the pavements as they shop for souvenirs and decide where to dine. On the left is Keswick Cafeteria and a branch of Timothy Whites, where films could be developed. The tall building is the *"Queen's Hotel"* which boasted all modern conveniences – including television – and also offered an inclusive daily charge for one's "servant or driver". Further up is *"Ye Olde Friars"* restaurant. In the centre is the moot hall with its one-handed clock and, on the right, are two more hotels and a garage with a petrol pump on the roadside. In the bottom right, beside a large sign advertising *"Lettered Rock"*, two visitors are making a most important decision – which postcards to buy from the wonderful selection on display! *(Published by G.P. Abraham Ltd., real photograph no. 89).*

Although these coaches, parked in Castle Square, Caernarvon, look fairly streamlined, they lacked the comfort and refinements of their modern equivalents. For schools, Sunday schools and other groups, the annual coach trip was an exciting day out to the seaside or places of interest. The coaches were allocated a special parking area close to the castle. On the corner is Aston's furniture shop and two doors along is the booking office for Crosville, the local bus company. At least these trippers have a lovely sunny day for their outing – and the coaches have their sun roofs open. *(Posted in Colwyn Bay, June 1959; published by Valentine, real photograph no. W6045).*

"Ooh, my back" could well be the words spoken by this coach driver! A tour of Dartmoor, with its lanes, hills and narrow bridges would have been very tiring for the drivers of these old coaches. Here, he is standing in the Square at Princetown while his passengers return to their seats. Many are stopping to make a fuss of the ponies; the photograph has been retouched – to remove all signs of pony droppings! Princetown was used to catering for tourists as many coaches and motorists stopped there for refreshments, souvenirs or to simply stretch their legs. *(Published by Harvey Barton Ltd, real photograph no. 43432).*

The British Commonwealth

In 1949, after India declared its intention to become a republic, a meeting of Commonwealth Heads of State agreed that republics could remain in the Commonwealth provided that the British Sovereign was acknowledged as "the symbol of the free association of its independent member nations and as such the head of the Commonwealth". Some British politicians were totally opposed to any reduction in the "wide-flung colonial Empire", whose peoples composed a quarter of the world's population. However, as the 1950s progressed, several colonies, previously ruled by Britain and other European nations, began their struggle for independence. Once it was realised that changes were inevitable, the British assisted with their colonies' transition to independent status within the Commonwealth.

These immaculate gardens and buildings of the "Tea Hotel" at Kericho, Kenya, are typical of the high standards of comfort and service expected by colonial settlers in the twentieth century. This was a Brooke Bond Hotel, situated in south-west Kenya, the major tea-growing area. This upland region was the main area of British settlement and was known as the "white highlands". The hotel obviously fulfilled expectations as the message reads:- "...one of the best hotels I've ever stayed in". The African colonies were particularly keen to become independent and the Gold Coast was first, gaining its independence – as Ghana – in 1957. Kenya's move to self-government was hindered by the Mau Mau rebellion of 1952-59, but was finally achieved in 1963. (posted at Nairobi in 1960).

There are plenty of British cars parked by the State Lottery Hall, in Salisbury, Southern Rhodesia. The Hall was built in 1938 and details of the lottery and draw dates are given on a board above the left-hand side of the building. From 1953 until 1962, the country was part of the Central African Federation. Independence was finally gained in 1980, since when the country has been known as Zimbabwe and Salisbury, the capital. as Harare. (published by Coombe & Dewar of Salisbury).

The people of Fiji were still proud to be a British colony and fly the Union Jack. This Fijian policeman in Suva, the capital, wears a uniform with a shirt similar to a British one. In 1953, the islands' total population was 289,000 and the enviable post of Governor was held by Sir Ronald Garvey who received an annual salary of £3250. The islands attained their independence within the Commonwealth in 1970. (Published by Stinsons, Suva; printed in England by J. Salmon Ltd., no.14).

More British cars are on this view of Shaws Building, Singapore. The building housed the Capitol Theatre and cinema which was showing the film The Lost Tribe starring Johnny Weismuller. The rest of the ground floor appears to be occupied by small shops. Singapore became a British Crown Colony in 1946 and then a self-governing state from 1957. (Published by J. Arthur Dixon on a 'Colorgravure' postcard).

During the 1950s British servicemen were stationed on Christmas Island, in the central Pacific Ocean, were working on the British hydrogen bomb project. An RAF Vickers Valiant dropped the first such bomb over the Pacific on 15th May 1957. Despite the nature of their work, the camp seems to be in an idyllic setting with the tents lining the Pacific shore. The card was sent by a serviceman in January 1959 and has a British stamp, cancelled with the Forces Post Office postmark for Christmas Island. (Published by Raphael Tuck).

For British servicemen posted overseas, one well-used link with their families was the weekly radio programme Family Favourites, broadcast by the BBC on Sundays, with presenters Jean Metcalfe and Cliff Michelmore. This card shows Cyprus and was posted by a British serviceman stationed there in 1959. A state of emergency had been declared in 1955 because of the guerrilla war between the Greek and Turkish factions. A draft constitution was drawn up in 1957 and the new republic was declared in 1960. (Published by Raphael Tuck, no.65).

World Events

In the USA, the first session to be held in the new United Nations building was on 27th February 1952. The building was erected on a site donated by John D. Rockefeller, to a design by an international committee of architects. The card shows President Eisenhower addressing a meeting of the Eighth Session of the Assembly, on 8th December 1953. Seated behind him are Mme V. Pandit, President of the General Assembly; Dag Hammarskjold, Secretary-General and Andrew Cordier, Executive Assistant. *(United Nations postcard no.P7305).*

Also in the USA, at Anaheim, California, Disneyland opened its gates to the public on 18th July 1955. Walt Disney had conceived the idea of a family park, where parents and children could have fun together in pleasant surroundings. It had taken many years and many changes of plan before he was satisfied with its design. From the start, this 160-acre park attracted crowds of over 5 million "guests" a year. *(Posted in Los Angeles, February 1957; published by Disneyland).*

"Never before in history has so much hope for so many people been gathered together in a single organization. Your deliberations and decisions during these somber years have already realized part of those hopes."
— PRESIDENT EISENHOWER

In Brussels, the Universal and International Expo ran from 17th April to 19th October 1958. Its main theme was "nuclear energy working for peace". This theme is also reflected in the structure of the main pavilion – the Atomium – seen on the left of this novelty postcard. On the right, the "canvas" on the artist's easel also shows the Atomium through a sheet of green cellophane; however, when this is pulled up by means of the thumb notch, a red sheet of cellophane covers the easel and the Mannekin Pis is seen. The cellophane is placed between the two sides of the card which is constructed like a sealed envelope. When the Exposition was dismantled, the Atomium was retained. It towers over the surrounding parkland, being 335ft high, with each sphere having a diameter of 69ft. *(Published by Ch. Lalieu, no.8A).*

In 1956 the British Astronomer Royal declared that the concept of space travel was "bilge"! Despite his discouraging remarks, the latter years of the fifties were dominated by the "space race" between the USA and the USSR. The first successful launch of an artificial satellite was Russia's *Sputnik 1* on 4th October 1957. The satellite was a sphere with four aerials and transmitted signals to Earth for 21 days. On 3rd November 1957, *Sputnik 2* carried the first living creature into space – Laika the dog. Her flight provided data on the effect of weightlessness on living organisms. Laika died – painlessly – when her oxygen ran out after 7 days. The Americans, meanwhile, had problems with their rockets; their first attempt in December 1957 failed when their Vanguard rocket exploded on take off. However, they successfully launched the satellite *Explorer 1* in February 1958; this grapefruit-sized satellite led to the discovery of the Van Allen radiation belts. In 1959 the Russians launched their *Luna* series of spacecraft; *Luna 1* went beyond the moon and into solar orbit; *Luna 2* impacted on the moon and *Luna 3* passed behind the moon and sent back pictures of the far side. The Russians also managed to send animals into space and return them, alive, to Earth. This is a Russian card, issued for the International Geophysical Year in 1958. It shows Laika with *Sputniks 1, 2 and 3*. The race to put a man on the moon was under way!

Fifties miscellany

In 1955, faced with death duties of over £4 million, the young Duke of Bedford opened Woburn Abbey to the public. On opening day, a visitor was found snipping a piece out of the curtains – as a souvenir! By 1958, more experienced but still anxious to attract much-needed funds, the Duke toured the USA, lecturing on historical England, its buildings and etiquette. A year later he attended a private showing of a nudist film, part of which had been filmed at Woburn; he commented, *"I don't care as long as it brings money..."*. Eventually he managed to turn his house into a successful business venture attracting vast numbers of visitors. On the card he is shown with a deer from the park in which the house is situated. *(Printed for his Grace the Duke of Bedford by Dennis Productions, Newcolour no. 3406).*

From the mid-1950s blocks of flats were built in many British towns and cities in an effort to solve the housing problem. Before this time there had been planning restrictions limiting the height of such buildings to 100ft or ten storeys. These flats are on the Tile Hill estate in Coventry. There are three 11-storey blocks of 99 two-bedroom flats, plus a shopping area, public buildings and schools. New building methods and materials and the invention of the tower crane to carry out the work encouraged councils to erect high-rise buildings. They had the advantage of being economical in land and, from 1956, extra government housing subsidies were paid for buildings over six storeys high – this rose, storey by storey, encouraging councils to build higher and higher! The British skyline was changed for ever! *(Posted in Coventry, April 1960; published by Gordon Fraser, real photograph no. ATO2-9).*

LONDON LIFE: An East End Rag-and-Bone Man. Crockery is offered as an alternative to cash.

The Rag-and-Bone man provided a useful service to householders and industry alike. On his regular rounds, he collected rags, bones, scrap metal and other items of junk which were sold to industry for recycling. As he toured the streets, he announced his presence with a shout that was instantly recognised. People who had stuff for him received either cash or crockery in exchange. *(Published by Charles Skilton Ltd,. London Life no.11).*

Post-war housing estates differed from those built before World War 2. Town planning – a new profession – was to control the density and layout of any development. Instead of rows of identical houses, some variety was encouraged so that houses would be at varying distances from the roads and would have different features from those of their immediate neighbours. This estate at Aveley, Essex, shows a variety in the layout of porches, windows and roofs. They were obviously new when this view was taken, as the builder's board is still standing at the far end of the lay-by. The right-hand side seems to be undeveloped and only half of the shops are occupied. In 1953, the Housing Minister, Harold MacMillan, was able to announce that they had exceeded their target for new houses with 301,000 new houses being completed in a year. *(Published by Frith, real photograph no. ALY.19).*

This aerial view must have been taken shortly after the completion of Claerwen Dam in 1952. There is much evidence of construction work in the foreground with temporary buildings and earth-moving equipment dwarfed by the huge dam. This was the fourth dam to be built in the Elan Valley and was the largest in Britain. The reservoirs supply water to the West Midlands by a 73-mile aqueduct. *(Published by Valentine, real photograph no. W190, and posted at Newtown, Montgomeryshire in August 1958).*

"MUVVER'S HAVING A **DIZZY** SPELL!"
"OH—I'M SORRY TO HEAR
THAT SHE'S ILL!"
"SHE ISN'T—SHE'S JUST FALLEN
IN THE SPIN DRYER!"

=== A 'BAMFORTH' COMIC ===

As the decade went by, British reservoirs had to cope with ever-increasing demands for water. Homes were better equipped with hot and cold running water, flushing toilets and proper bathrooms. People also needed water for laundry, cleaning their new cars and for the gardens that were laid at most new houses. The latest electrical domestic appliances were a great boon to the busy housewife – who now often had a job outside the home as well. Washing machines took the drudgery out of the household laundry. However, most families still relied on fine weather to dry the washing, whilst the lucky few had a spin dryer. It was typical of the artist at Bamforth's to see the funny side of things and create comic designs from such everyday tasks! *(Posted in September 1960; published by Bamforth no.1601).*

"I WARNED YOU THAT THE STRONG **SUCTION** WOULD AMAZE YOU LADY!"

=== A 'BAMFORTH' COMIC ===

The growth in women's employment meant that many families had an increased standard of living. Some households were fortunate enough to be able to save the wife's earnings for extras such as holidays, cars, furnishings and electrical goods. Fitted carpets replaced linoleum when new man-made fibres and modern machinery resulted in a wide range of cheaper floorcoverings. In turn, this meant that households needed a vacuum cleaner to look after their carpets and sales of these appliances increased rapidly throughout the decade. *(Posted in July 1958; published by Bamforth no.1426).*

HER MAJESTY QUEEN MARY'S CARPET

This unique and beautiful carpet was certainly too valuable to be "hoovered". It was the handiwork of the elderly Queen Mary who completed the carpet in January 1950. It was worked in grospoint needlework and contains over a million stitches; measuring 10ft by 7ft, it had taken her eight years of hard work. She presented the carpet to the nation to be sold as a contribution to the dollar export drive, believing that "it is the duty of every individual to contribute something directly to help the country in its need for dollars." The carpet was displayed at the Victoria and Albert Museum where 90,000 visitors paid 6d (2½p) to see it. The proceeds from the sale of this postcard went towards the expenses of the sale of the carpet. It was then taken to the U.S.A. – on board the *Queen Mary* – where 400,000 people admired the Queen's handiwork; this raised a further $100,000. The sum of £35,354 was eventually passed to the British Exchequer being the proceeds of the exhibitions and sale of the carpet.